# YORKSHIRE POTTERIES, POTS AND POTTERS

# YORKSHIRE POTTERIES, POTS AND POTTERS

BY

## OXLEY GRABHAM, M.A., M.B.O.U.
### LATE KEEPER OF THE YORK MUSEUM

*With a new Introduction by*
## PETER WALTON

Republished by S.R. Publishers Ltd., 1971
First published in York, 1916

© 1971 S.R. Publishers Limited,
East Ardsley, Wakefield,
Yorkshire, England.

ISBN 0 85409 659 0

Reprinted in England by Scolar Press Ltd.,
Menston, Yorkshire, U.K.

# INTRODUCTION

North Staffordshire has long been one of the main centres of ceramic manufacture in this country. One of the most famous of the other important centres was Yorkshire, particularly South Yorkshire. It is becoming more and more apparent that the potteries of Yorkshire rivalled, both in size and in the quality of their products, those of Staffordshire.

In Yorkshire, as in Staffordshire, the earthenware rather than the porcelain tradition was strong in the eighteenth century. The great Staffordshire porcelain factories reached their height in the nineteenth century, with the notable exception of Longton Hall. Yorkshire's great porcelain factory, the Rockingham Works at Swinton made porcelain of a high quality in the second quarter of the nineteenth century. There is no evidence to suggest that tin-glazed earthenware was made either in Staffordshire or Yorkshire, although there is apparently a tradition that 'delftware', as it is usually called in England, was made at Leeds. If delftware had been made in Yorkshire one would expect to find a strong tradition of painting on Yorkshire pottery, but in fact, as in the case of Staffordshire pottery, there is little painting until the middle of the eighteenth century. At this time enamelling shops were established in Leeds. The firm of Robinson and Rhodes were responsible for most of the early enamelling, not only on Leeds salt-glaze and creamware, but on Wedgwood creamware as well. The Slipware tradition rather than a tradition of painting was strong in early Yorkshire pottery and fine peasant slipwares were made in the Halifax and Huddersfield areas until the late nineteenth century. Slip was also used to decorate 'pearlware' in the early nineteenth century and very good use of this technique was made by the potteries of South Yorkshire and the potteries on the Humber.

Francis Place of York was possibly a pioneer of salt-glazed stoneware, experimenting with stoneware contemporaneously with John Dwight of Fulham. The brown salt-glazed stonewares of the type made at Fulham and Nottingham were made in Yorkshire and recent excavations have produced shards which suggest that a fine white salt-glazed stoneware was made by a number of Yorkshire potteries apart from that known to have been made at Leeds and Swinton. The other main types of ware made in Staffordshire — the unglazed red-ware, tortoise-shell and the other wares decorated with coloured glazes were also made in Yorkshire, until about 1780. An earthenware with a green glaze of the type associated with the North Staffordshire 'cauliflower wares' was made popular by the potteries at Swinton and Mexborough in the Regency period. 'Pearlware' — a very white earthenware with a bluish glaze developed by Wedgwood — was made at Leeds from about 1785 and was a very characteristic product of many other Yorkshire potteries. But perhaps the Yorkshire potters are best known for their cream-coloured earthenwares, and that made by the Leeds Pottery especially, rivalled the 'Queensware' produced by Wedgwood. The problems of attributing cream-coloured earthenwares to particular factories have always been great and the pattern books are therefore very important. The Leeds Pattern Book (c.1814 edition) reprinted in Donald Towner's *The Leeds Pottery* in 1963 and the pattern book published by David Dunderdale and Co. of the Castleford Pottery are useful tools in the process of attribution. It is illuminating to compare the Yorkshire pattern books with those published in other manufacturing centres. For instance, one published for James and Charles Whitehead of Hanley in 1798 contains many designs which are almost identical to those in the Leeds Pattern Book.

Black basaltes, employed by the Wedgwood and Bentley partnership in Staffordshire to make ornamental wares, was a ceramic material used a great deal in Yorkshire in the early nineteenth century mainly for useful wares. Another stoneware often associated with Yorkshire, and with Castleford in particular is a white feldspathic stoneware best known in the form of teapots. Stonewares were used to manufacture that very characteristic class of nineteenth century pottery, the decorative jug. In Staffordshire, this type, at its best, was made by firms like Ridgways, Charles Meigh and Son's and Mintons. In Yorkshire good examples were made at Swinton. The late nineteenth and early twentieth centuries saw the rise of factories specialising in 'Art Pottery'. Yorkshire had its fair share of these. The best was probably the Linthorpe Pottery at Middlesbrough which produced designs by Christopher Dresser. The Burmantofts Art Pottery at Leeds made pots decorated with coloured glazes of the type often called 'majolica' as well as painted earthenware.

The collecting and serious study of English pottery began in the middle of the nineteenth century. Joseph Marryat's *Collections towards a history of pottery and porcelain*, which contained one of the first surveys of English pottery, was published in 1850. The pottery of Yorkshire received only scant mention and the first significant scholarly contribution to the history of the Yorkshire factories was made by Llewylln Jewitt in his monumental survey of British Ceramics in 1878. Oxley Grabham records his debt to Jewitt in the preface to *Yorkshire Potteries, Pots and Potters*. The Leeds Pottery received much attention in the late nineteenth century culminating in the publication of the early monograph *Historical Notices of the Leeds Old Pottery* by Joseph and Frank Kidson in 1892. This was superseded by Donald Towner's book *The Leeds Pottery*, which is the modern authority, in 1963.

Lady Charlotte Schreiber, one of the great early collectors, who began collecting English ceramics in about 1865, possessed some Yorkshire Pottery, (now in the Victoria and Albert Museum), and by the turn of the century there were a number of important collections, mainly in the North. One of these, formed by Thomas Boynton of Bridlington, is now at the Yorkshire Museum in York. Thomas Boynton was one of those responsible for beginning the now excellent collection of Yorkshire pottery in that Museum. Arthur Hurst, another collector and benefactor of the Yorkshire Museum, wrote the catalogue of the Boynton Collection (published in 1922), which was an important contribution to the study of Yorkshire Pottery. Another important early account, by Dr. Maud Sellers, appeared in Volume II of the *Victoria County History* in 1912. Oxley Grabham presented his report to the Yorkshire Philosophical Society in 1915 and it was later reprinted in its present form. This useful little book appeared during the same period as a number of other regional studies. For instance, one by Celia Henry of Sussex Pottery was published in two articles in the Connoisseur in 1909 and 1912. Oxley Grabham was a Keeper of the York Museum and had access to some of the great collections of Yorkshire pottery. He also had the advantage of being close to an oral tradition and he was able to interview ex-workmen from some of the potteries. His account, therefore, contains some important source material.

The collecting and study of Yorkshire pottery has more recently enjoyed a revival. There have been a number of excavations which have added greatly to our knowledge. Some of the results of recent research have already been published, and in the next few years we may expect a number of important publications to appear. It is felt, however, that although much material in Oxley Grabham's book is now out of date and possibly misleading, it is nevertheless a source work and provides the groundwork for future studies. It is hoped that this reprint will make what is now rather a scarce book, available to many more people.

Peter Walton

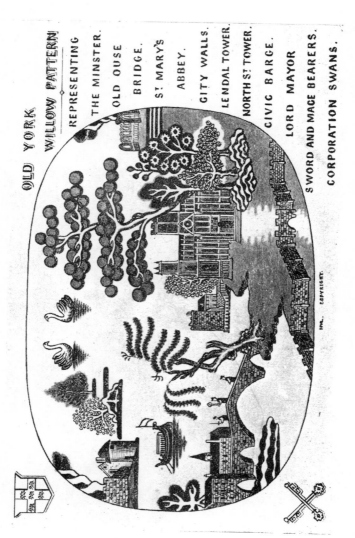

OLD YORK
WILLOW PATTERN

REPRESENTING

THE MINSTER.

OLD OUSE
BRIDGE.

S.ᵗ MARY'S
ABBEY.

CITY WALLS.

LENDAL TOWER.

NORTH S.ᵗ TOWER.

CIVIC BARGE.

LORD MAYOR

SWORD AND MACE BEARERS.

CORPORATION SWANS.

*By Mr H. M. Loadman.*

# YORKSHIRE POTTERIES, POTS AND POTTERS.

## BY

### OXLEY GRABHAM, M.A., M.B.O.U.,

Keeper of the York Museum.

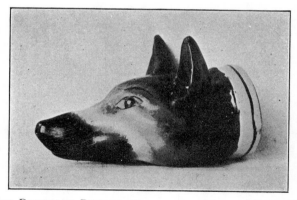

LEEDS RHYTON OR DRINKING CUP IN THE FORM OF A FOX'S MASK.

# PREFACE.

STRICTLY speaking, under the above heading, one ought to include the vast amount of pottery which was made in the broad-acred county during the ancient British, the Roman, the Saxon, and the Mediæval periods. But to do this properly would, unfortunately, more than double or treble the space at my command. Indeed, as it is, the difficulty has been to compress what I had to say within the limits of this paper, which only deals with Yorkshire Pottery as it is known to Collectors. For a good many years I have been much interested in the subject, and I think what first started me was being the possessor of a small collection, which came to me from my forbears.

I have taken infinite pains in getting together my information. I have hunted up old men who have worked at the various potteries, have visited the sites of most of the potteries dealt with, and have taken photographs of some of them, and have been in communication with many collectors and others who were interested in the subject; but, even so, I am only too conscious of many sins of omission and commission, but I have done my best, and I trust that my critics will let me down lightly. This I will say, that it is no easy matter to hunt up the particular information one wants about long forgotten people and places, and it has taken me a very considerable time to do so, yet I have enjoyed the work, and have obtained much instruction and amusement in the process.

Thanks to the initiative many years ago, of Mr. Thomas Boynton, of Bridlington, and the late Canon Raine, of York, the foundations of a fine Collection were got together in the York Museum. This has regularly been added to, both by gift and purchase, until at the present time we possess a series of Yorkshire Pottery which will be very bad to beat, if indeed it can be equalled elsewhere.

Mr. Thomas Boynton himself is the owner of a magnificent Collection, and I gratefully acknowledge his unvarying kindness and assistance to me when I was but a raw amateur. Mr. Arthur Hurst, York, also possesses a very fine Collection of Yorkshire Pottery; he has been a most generous donor to ours, and I am indebted to him for much help and advice in this particular branch of my studies.

Mr. Richard Wilson, of Armley, Leeds, has the best Collection of Leeds Ware in existence, and he has most kindly allowed me to thoroughly examine his treasures.

I must also express my best thanks to Mr. Bowman Heald, of the Kilnhurst Pottery, and to Mr Nicholas Taylor, late of the Denholme Pottery, for much historical information concerning the various potteries in their districts; to Dr. Maud Sellers who wrote the article on "Yorkshire Pottery" for the *Victoria County History*; to Mr. J. R. Triffitt, York, who has kindly presented us with several pieces from his own Collection; to the late Mr. Riley, Bramley, nr. Leeds; to Mr. William Cooper, Aislaby Hall, Pickering; to Dr. Kirk, Hungate Hall, Pickering; to Archdeacon H. Armstrong Hall; to Mr. Baker Hudson, the Dorman Memorial Museum, Middlesbrough; to Mr. R. Bond, Burmantofts Works; to Mr. T. Coates, Burton-in-Lonsdale; to Mr. Sidney Hawley, Rotherham; to Mr. P. Crossley, Commondale Works; to Mr. P. Graham, Clarence Potteries, Norton, Stockton-on-Tees; to Mr. H. Armstrong, Stockton; and many others who have so kindly assisted me in my labours, and last but by no means least, my best thanks are due to Mr. William Watson, the Museum, York, for the great care and trouble he has taken in preparing most of the excellent photographs with which this paper is illustrated.

To Mr. H. M. Loadman, Stonegate, York, I am greatly indebted for the loan of the two blocks representing respectively the York " Willow " pattern and the ordinary " Willow " pattern. The former, shown on the frontispiece, is a most ingenious idea of Mr. Loadman's, and if a service of plates were made showing this particular pattern, they would be of very considerable interest.

The best account of Yorkshire Pottery in general is to be found in Llewellynn Jewitt's "Ceramic Art of Great Britain," and I have drawn upon his pages for much otherwise unobtainable information.

The classic work on Leeds Pottery is that by Messrs. Joseph R. and Frank Kidson, and those who would know more of that most famous pottery cannot do better than read what these authors have to say upon the subject. I am indebted to them for much information.

The article on " Yorkshire Pottery," with many illustrations, by Dr. Maud Sellers, in the *Victoria County History*, Vol. II., is well worthy of perusal by all who are interested in this subject.

All the Potteries described are arranged in alphabetical order.

## ERRATUM.

The Leech Jar belonging to Dr. J. L. Kirk, Pickering, Fig. 54, p. 63, has been found on closer examination to be of Wedgwood's make and *not* Leeds, but I have seen one very similar, marked LEEDS POTTERY.

# YORKSHIRE POTTERIES, POTS, AND POTTERS.

## BRADSHAW HEAD POTTERY.

Situated near Denholme, this pottery was started about the year 1835, by two Catheralls, grandsons of old Jonathan Catherall, of the Soil Hill Pottery. It was closed down for good after working for two years.

## BURMANTOFTS POTTERY.

Clay goods were first made at these works in the year 1858, and previous to this coal and ironstone mining was carried on. Burmantofts Pottery was quite unknown up to as recently as 1882. The Burmantofts Works, near Leeds, now the property of the Leeds Fire-clay Co. Ltd., were up to that time principally engaged in the production of salt-glazed sanitary pipes, fire-bricks and quarries, salt-glazed bricks, etc. Mr. R. Bond, the works manager, who has very kindly given me all the information in his power about these works, tells me that the year 1882 saw the first attempted production of pottery, and art pottery in its best sense. From the beginning the greatest care was exercised in order to ensure accuracy of work produced on the thrower's wheel, the outline of each article receiving most careful attention before it was permitted to go to the hands of the operator. The effect of this great care was soon evidenced by the demand from the important firms in the trade for this ware.

Burmantofts Pottery found its way into the best houses, and was called for from all parts of the world. Probably the outstanding feature from the artistic point of view was the purity of the three principal colours produced, viz. : Persian blue, orange yellow, and sang-de-Bœuf. In addition to these however, there

were many blendings of colours on plain pottery, and a portion of
the plain pottery was also artistically treated in "slip" colours,
flowers being the chief decoration.    Later on, after much experi-
ment, Anglo-Persian pottery was introduced, the distinguishing
characteristic being its artistic colouring and effective design.    In
later years a popular demand was met by the production of
modelled pottery treated in one or more colours of great richness
of tone.    It was a great blow to the artistic side of the productions
of the city of Leeds that the manufacture had finally to be given
up for want of financial success, but the pieces now in existence
are much treasured by their fortunate possessors.    The making of
pottery was discontinued in August 1904.    The pottery will all be
found to be marked as per illustration, meaning " Burmantofts
Faience."

The works are now employed in making terra-cotta Faience,
which is a highly glazed and finished terra-cotta, made in all
colours; ornamental tiles, and glazed bricks in all colours.    A new
kind of terra-cotta called "Marmo" was made in 1908, and in
that year a building was erected in Coppergate, York, under Mr.
Whincup, faced with this material.

Since the year 1880 great strides have been made by the
successful adaptation of Faience to architectural work, and it is
now largely used for permanent adornment of public buildings,
principally of the Renaissance style.

The Burmantofts estate covers an area of about one hundred
acres, some fifteen of which are occupied by workshops and kilns.
Both the clay and the coal wherewith to bake it, are obtained on
the spot, the former lies two feet thick, one hundred yards from
the surface, under a fourteen inch seam of the Low Moor Better
Bed coal, and covers about one hundred acres.    It is sent up in
rock-like blocks, requiring to be crushed and sifted by machinery,
but is extremely plastic and tenacious and contracts but little in
drying, will bear great heat, and when burnt preserves its hard-
ness and exactness of form, solidity under pressure, and clearness
of colour.    A very large number of hands are employed here in
the pits and various workshops, and in the studios a staff of

artists is constantly engaged. The whole of the designs as well as the articles made from them, are produced on the premises.

Fig. 1. BURMANTOFTS POTTERY. ("SPLASHED WARE.")
York Museum Collection.

## THE BURTON POTTERIES.

Burton-in-Lonsdale is a little village lying on the north bank of the river Greta, in the north-west of Yorkshire. Its nearest railway stations are Bentham, about three miles away, Ingleton about three miles, and Kirby Lonsdale, about six miles away.

There are in all five potteries in Burton, and about the same number are said to have been done away with in years gone by, some of the old ones having been substituted by new ones. The old manufacturers' names still remembered are Cornelius Gibson, Wilson, Bradshaw, Burton, Baggaley, Kilburn, Batty, and Greenip. The wares made are bread mugs, milk bowls cooking dishes and pots, plant pots, various articles for domestic use, jam jars, bottles, etc., in black, brown, and white glazes. It would be a great boon to these flourishing little potteries if a branch line could be made to the village to relieve the very great inconvenience of carting the goods to and from the stations.

The following are the five Burton potteries :—

**Town End Pottery,** manufacturing black and brown ware, etc., was worked by a Thomas Bateson in the early part of the 18th century, and some think there was a Gibson before him. Thomas Bateson was succeeded by John Bateson, and he in turn by another Thomas Bateson. The last of the four generations was Richard Bateson. This terminates the Batesons at the Town End Pottery about 1853, when a William Parker took up the business, and it is now worked by his brother John Parker.

**Baggaley Pottery** was established about 1750, and was worked for many years by Baggaley. He was a relation of the mother of the present owner, Mr. Thomas Coates, who most kindly supplied me with much information about these potteries and who still works the pottery, manufacturing black, brown, and white glazes, plant pots, tobacco jars, etc.

**Greta Bank Pottery** was established in 1850 and has been worked by Mr. T. Burton, a Mr. Greenets, a Mr. Parker, and is now worked by Mr. G. Kilshaw, manufacturing black and brown wares, etc.

Fig. 2.   BURTON WARE.   Baggaley Pottery.   York Museum Collection.

**Bridge End Pottery** was the first stoneware pottery in Burton, was worked by William Bateson in 1830, and after many years it came into the possession of Mr. T. Coates, and was worked by him as a stoneware pottery nntil the year 1906, when he sold out to a Robert Bateson, a dissolving partner from the Waterside Pottery.

**Waterside Pottery** was built as a stoneware pottery by John Bateson about 1840, he was a great uncle to the present Messrs. Harry and Frank Bateson, who are still carrying on the business. This is the largest pottery in Burton.

The stoneware potteries manufacture bottles, cooking pots, jam jars, etc.

## CASTLEFORD POTTERY.

This pottery was established about 1780 by David Dunderdale, of whom the best description is given by Archdeacon H. A. Hall, B.D.,[*] as follows: David Dunderdale was born at the " Crosse," Briggate, Leeds, on January 9th, 1772, and was baptised at St. John's on the 21st of February. He could not have been more than twenty years of age when he embarked upon the venture at Castleford, for in 1796 a pattern book was issued—not necessarily the first—of which a copy was exhibited by Mr. Richard Wilson, of Armley, near Leeds, at the Old Leeds Exhibition, held at the City Art Gallery, from July 24th to September 24th, 1908.

This pattern book is in French and Spanish, the title page running :—

" Desseins des pieces de Fayence fabriquèes à Castleford
Pottery prés de Leeds par Dd. Dunderdale et Co.
Dibuxos de las piezas de Lozaque se fabrican a Castleford
Pottery cerca de Leeds par Dd. Dunderdale y Co.
1796."

Of this pattern book it is sufficient to say that it is a colourable imitation, so far as size and general idea are concerned, of the Leeds books, but the drawing and production are very inferior. It contains fifty-seven pages of designs and seven pages of indices, but unfortunately there is no descriptive letterpress. The factory certainly prospered for a time. Dunderdale took into partnership a Mr. Plowes, who however deserted to Ferrybridge, and subsequently Thos. Ed. Upton, Thos Russell - a Harrogate innkeeper— and John Bramley, who was probably a relative of his wife, whose maiden name was Ann Bramley. He lived at Dunford House,

---

*Vide* " Handbook of the Old Leeds Exhibition, 1908," p. 39, *et seq.*, " The greater part of the very fine collection of David Dunderdale's Ware, got together by Archdeacon Hall, has been acquired by Mr. Arthur Hurst, East Lodge, St. Peter's Grove, York, and through the kindness of that gentleman is now on view in the York Museum."

Methley, " a good mansion house " close to and on the east of the
road leading to Methley Bridge, which had been built by Michael
Stocks of Methley, fifty years previously, in front of a very ancient
and historic tenement, bearing the same name.

Dunderdale was churchwarden and overseer of the poor for
Methley at various periods between 1799 and 1814, and he was a
First-Lieutenant of the Pontefract Volunteers of 1798-9 (of which
the Hon. Henry Savile was Major and the Hon. Chas. Savile and
John, Earl of Mexborough, were then Captains), from all of which
we may gather that at this period the works were doing well.
The Peninsular War came, however, as a death blow to enterprises
which depended to any extent upon the French and Spanish
markets. French privateers roamed the seas, and cargo after
cargo of the Castleford wares fell, as it is asserted, into the hands
of the enemy. At home there was neither money to purchase, nor
artistic enthusiasm to support, anything superior to the commonest
productions. David Dunderdale retired from the works—it is
hinted with sadly diminished resources—soon after the Peace, and
died at Trafalgar Street, Leeds, in May, 1824, aged 52 ; he is
buried with his parents in St. John's churchyard, and is described
on the slab which covers their remains as " late of Dunford House."

In 1820 the manufactory was closed, and in 1821 a part of the
works was taken by some of the workmen. They were succeeded
by Taylor, Harrison and Co., Harrison having been an apprentice
of Dunderdale's. These works were an offshoot of the old Pottery.
At the close of the year 1825, the old works were taken by Asquith,
Wood and Co. They were joined in partnership by Thomas
Nicholson from the Leeds Pottery, and carried on the business
as Asquith, Wood and Nicholson, and afterwards as Wood and
Nicholson alone. In 1854 another change took place by which
Mr. Nicholson, one of the old firm, retained the works, and took
into partnership Thomas Hartley, the style of the firm being
Thomas Nicholson and Co. When Mr. Nicholson retired it was
carried on by T. Hartley alone, and afterwards with partners
under the old name of Nicholson and Co. In December, 1871,
Mr. Hartley died, and the Castleford Pottery was then, and still
is, carried on by his co-partners, Messrs. Hugh McDowall Clokie
and John Masterman, under the style of " Clokie and Masterman."

The wares made in Dunderdale's time consisted :—

First—of useful table pottery, dinner services, etc., well moulded
and potted ; the glaze where it has accumulated in any quantity

shows the greenish tinge, so often observed in the Leeds Pottery, denoting arsenic. The very popular " Willow " pattern differs in some respects from the Leeds design. One pattern which I have never seen on any other ware but Castleford has two figures on it, one riding on an animal with horns, evidently meant for Buddha and the sacred cow. We have several examples of this in the York Museum.

The feather-edge pattern was also used here, as it was at Leeds, etc.

Second—cream or Queen's ware. It was, as Archdeacon Hall points out, in this line that the greatest imitation of the Leeds manufacture took place. The Hartley family of Methley and Kippax was not improbably connected with that which made the Leeds Pottery famous, and it is easy to understand that workmen would go from one factory to another, taking with them designs and methods, according as wages and other inducements offered. Though there were inferior pieces of cream ware placed upon the market badly potted and badly designed, yet some of them are of great beauty, and very little, if at all, inferior to those for which Leeds was so famous. The " twig " baskets are good examples of this. A " trembleuse " or chocolate cup stand in our Collection is of inferior make, whilst one in Mr. Hurst's possession leaves little to be desired. One very rare piece in our Collection is a barber's or shaving bowl. It may be mentioned here that while in the case of the Leeds baskets and dishes the centre is almost always plain, that, in the ware of Castleford (and Wedgwood) is almost always filled in either by the pattern or by coloured crossed lines.

The pattern book shows the large range of cream ware offered by the factory.

Third—the black or basalt ware, consisting of tea sets made to be used at funerals. A beautiful jug with panels containing figures and decorated with leaves, and a sugar basin with figures on each side, are in Mr. Hurst's Collection. They were of a deeper and brighter black than those of Leeds.

Fourth—the vitreous semi-lucent ware so ably produced by David Dunderdale. Fine examples of the tea pots, etc., are in the Collections of Mr. Wilson, Mr. Hurst, and Mr. Boynton.

The white stoneware jugs and mugs made by Dunderdale in common with Adams, Turner, Wedgwood, and other great potters, have certain elements in common. The material is of similar composition, the neck and upper part of the handle are dark brown, the lower portion of the body is cane pattern, the middle portion bears figures, *e.g.*, hunting and rural scenes in relief. The Castleford products are of great merit, and are distinguished by the "grass" border on the shoulder, and the somewhat large foot, and the typical Castleford handle.

The Dr. Pratt or Barker ware jugs, made at Lane Delf, now Middle Fenton, from 1775 to 1810, are said to have been imitated here and at Leeds. These had zig-zag patterns or acanthus leaf decoration top and bottom, with sporting scenes in relief in colours round the body.

Archdeacon Hall further states that the genuine Castleford ware has, apart from the factory mark, several distinctive features: the " angles " are invariably recessed—concave not convex—and the ornament of the angles is what may be described as a line and dot pattern with lotus leaves below, the medallions and other applied ornaments are in low relief, and sometimes—as in the beautiful teapot belonging to Mr. Wilson—the ornaments are decorated in colour, the glaze shows green under the lid and at the bottom of the inside, and the handle is always that peculiar to Castleford.

A large trade was done with Spain, the Baltic, and other foreign parts. As has been pointed out many of the specimens turned out by Dunderdale are of great merit and beauty, and marked pieces are eagerly sought after by collectors.

The mark on these pieces is

|  |  |  |
|---|---|---|
| D. D. & Co. | | D. D. & Co. |
| CASTLEFORD | or | CASTLEFORD |
| | | POTTERY |

impressed in the ware.

The mark of the later proprietors when trading as T. Nicholson and Co. was a circular garter surmounted by a crown, and on the ribbon the initials of the firm, T. N. & Co., in the centre the name of the pattern. Personally I have never yet come across a piece so marked. The mark of the present firm is their initials within a border.

Mr. T. Boynton, Bridlington, has three obelisk-shaped ornaments of Castleford Parian ware. These are decorated on the bases with rustic landscapes and raised figures in classical style. The tops have sporting, musical, and warlike trophies on all the faces. The height of the largest is $11\frac{1}{2}$ ins., the smaller ones measure $9\frac{1}{2}$ ins.

Fig. 3.   BARBER'S OR SHAVING BOWL.   York Museum Collection.

Fig. 4.   TREMBLEUSE.   York Museum Collection.

Fig. 5. FRUIT DISH. York Museum Collection.

Fig. 6. TEAPOT. Mr. A. Hurst's Collection.

My brother has in his Collection a mug with the figure of a fighting cock upon it, and the words

POLLINGTON FOR EVER.　　made here.

Lord Pollington, the eldest son of the Earl of Mexborough, was M.P. for Pontefract in the years 1807, 1812, 1818, and 1820. In the election of August 15th, 1872, the then Lord Pollington was defeated by Mr. H. C. Childers, by 80 votes. This was the first Parliamentary election under the Ballot Act.

## COMMONDALE POTTERY.

Situated near Stokesley, these works were first started in the year 1861, under the name of the " Cleveland Fire Brick and Pottery Co. Ltd." The proprietor and first managing director was Mr. John Slater Pratt, printer, of Stokesley, who owned the land on which the works were erected, and who got the Company formed. Some York gentlemen were interested, among whom was Mr. Henry Hotham Newton, of the firm of Newton, Robinson and Brown, solicitors, now Brown and Elmhirst.

This Company ceased operations in 1867, and the works remained idle until 1872, when they were acquired by the late Mr. John Crossley, founder and first chairman of this Company. The manufacture of fine art and domestic pottery, properly speaking, was commenced by him in 1880, and continued by him until he turned over the works to a new Company, named " The Commondale Brick, Pipe and Pottery Co. Ltd." They continued the manufacture for some time, when the works were again closed down. They were next taken up by Mr. Thomas Ness, of Darlington, in the year 1893, trading as the " Commondale Brick and Pipe Co." After Mr. Ness's death, the works again passed into the hands of Messrs. Crossley, by whom they are still being carried on.

The manufacture of fine art and domestic pottery was discontinued about 1884, since which time nothing of this kind has been made, and the kilns for burning the same have been dismantled. The goods now made comprise stoneware pipes and sanitary ware of the highest class, architectural terra-cotta in red and buff, and vitrified adamantine paving bricks for paving purposes. The only things of ornamental character, apart from the architectural terra-cotta, are now garden vases and pedestals, made in both colours.

Marked pieces of this ware are now of great rarity. We have a teapot and two goblets with a very dark brownish black glaze, splashed and blotched with greyish green, also a terra-cotta tobacco jar with white beading top and bottom, the lid with a broad band of light blue near the white beading along the edge, and a large patch of blue on the knob. These are marked on the bottom, COMMONDALE POTTERY, the letters being arranged in a circle, impressed.

Fig. 7.   TEAPOT AND TWO GOBLETS.   York Museum Collection.

Fig. 8.   TOBACCO JAR.   York Museum Collection.

Mr. Hurst has a water-bottle, stopper. and stand in rich buff terra-cotta.   The stand is marked

CROSSLEY

COMMONDALE

Mr. P. Crossley, to whom I am indebted for most of the above account of the pottery, very kindly presented to us some years ago an orange-brown jug, ornamented with a group of figures on each side, and a vine—leaves and grapes—all in low relief.   This piece is unmarked.

# DENABY POTTERY.

This was started as a pottery in 1864 by Wilkinson and Wardle, the latter being a thoroughly practical potter, previously with the well knowh firm of Alcocks and Co., Burslem, Staffordshire. A very fine quality of the usual domestic earthenware in white, sponged, and printed ware was produced, but continual experiments in the manufacture did not conduce to commercial success, and the works were closed in 1870. Denaby was the most easterly of the south Yorkshire potteries, and was advantageously situated, being close to the Denaby Main Colliery, and having a siding into the works from the South Yorkshire, now the Great Central Railway Co. Distance from Mexboro' 1½ miles, and from Doncaster, 5½ miles. Subsequently the pottery was converted into a bone and glue works, but this in turn was closed, and for many years no work of any kind has been carried on, and there is nothing left to remind one that it ever was a pottery. A few years before the business was discontinued, it was carried on under the style of "Wardle and Co." or "John Wardle and Co.," Mr. W. Wilkinson withdrawing, and a Mr. Blyth, a mining engineer, taking his place as a partner of Wardle, who throughout was the practical potter in the concern.

Fig. 10.
MARK ON THE PLATE.

Fig. 9.   PLATE.   Mr. O. Grabham's Collection.

Marked pieces of Denaby Pottery are of extreme rarity. I have only seen one, and that was kindly given to me some years ago by Mr. Bowman Heald, of the Kilnhurst Pottery; it is a fine plate, with birds of paradise, groups of flowers and foliage, printed in a peculiar shade of blue on a white ground. The mark, printed on the bottom, is the Staffordshire knot, with

JOHN   WARDLE   &   CO.

above, and

NEAR   ROTHERHAM

## DENABY   POTTERY.

below. Another mark was the same knot, with the initials

W. W.   DENABY   POTTERY

and Jewitt gives the same knot with the words

WILKINSON & WARDLE. DENABY POTTERIES.

## DENHOLME POTTERY.

This pottery was established between 1780 and 1790 by Samuel Catherall, son of Jonathan Catherall of the Soil Hill Pottery, and this was continued by the family until August, 1893, when Mr. Nicholas Taylor purchased the same. He gave up the pottery in 1907, but for a year or two after this date, worked with a small kiln in the old Wesleyan chapel at Denholme. Mr. Taylor marked some of his most particular pieces, "N. Taylor, Denholme," in incised writing letters on the bottom of the ware. I have an inkstand so marked, in the so-called "Snail Horn" ware, made at all these South Yorkshire potteries, yellow and brown, giving a sort of striped and banded appearance.

The usual slip decorated articles, puzzle jugs, etc., were made here with a light and a very dark brown glaze, almost black, the same as in the other South Yorkshire coarse ware potteries. We have several pieces in our Collection.

# DON POTTERY.

This pottery, closely adjoining the canal at Swinton on which it had a wharf, was established in a very small way about 1790, and considerably increased in 1800 by John Green, of Newhill. He was one of the Greens, of Leeds, of the same family as the proprietors of the Leeds Pottery, and a proprietor in the Swinton property and pottery. He is in fact stated to have been the manager of the Leeds and Swinton Potteries, and to have sustained considerable losses on the breaking out of the French war.

About 1800 or a little later, he purchased a plot of almost waste and swampy ground at Swinton, and with the aid of partners set about the erection of the fine Don Works. At this time a man of the name of Newton had an enamel kiln at the back of his house at Swinton, where he used to burn such wares as he decorated. To this man for the first twelve months Green, of the Don Pottery brought his pattern pieces to be fired as he prepared them. In 1807, other members of the family united with John Green, who also had partners named Clarke, the firm trading as Greens, Clarke and Co. In 1831 Mr. Green was proprietor of the Don Pottery. In 1834 the pottery passed by purchase to Mr. Samuel Barker, of the Mexborough Pottery, which latter works he closed in 1844, and confined his operations entirely to the Don manufactory.

In 1851 the firm became "Samuel Barker and Son," the proprietors being Mr. Henry Barker and Mr. Edward Barker. This business which had been worked by the Barker family for nearly fifty years was transferred in November, 1882, by the proprietor, Mr. Edward Barker, the youngest son of Samuel Barker, to Messrs. Smith, Adamson, Wilkinson and Scorah, who carried it on under the old style of " Samuel Barker and Son."

For some years after this a very large volume of trade was done, principally for the London and export markets.

Messrs. Wilkinson and Scorah after about four years trading withdrew from the partnership, and Smith and Adamson continued alone, still trading as " Samuel Barker and Son." At the end of the eighties however, the trade began to languish, and in 1893 the works were finally set down. The goods, material, engravings, and general stock-in-trade were sold off later in the year (under liquidation), and the pottery, the freehold of which was retained by the Barker family, remained closed and tenantless until March,

1897, when the landlord's fixtures including engines, boilers, flint milling plant, machinery, etc., were disposed of by public auction, and shortly afterwards the works and land were sold in separate lots, and in due time two or three streets of shops and houses were erected on the site of the pottery.

The outer cases of two of the kilns nearest the canal were still standing in 1908, when I photographed them, having been converted into warehouses, etc.

Fig. 11.  RUINS OF THE DON POTTERY, 1908.

In its best days the Don Pottery probably turned out more goods than any other pottery in the county, except Leeds. It consisted of eight large kilns or ovens, namely, three "biscuits" and five "glosts."

Formerly in Samuel Barker's time an enormous export trade was done with Constantinople.

At the sale all the old models, blocks, cases, etc., which had made the works famous in its earlier years were sold in one lot, and were purchased by Mr. Bowman Heald and removed to the Kilnhurst Pottery.

One of the most remarkable of the early specimens of the ware produced here is a jug, commonly known as the "Jumper Jug," it is of great rarity, one specimen being in the possession of Mr. Thomas Boynton, Bridlington, where I have had the pleasure of examining it, along with many other beautiful specimens of York-shire Pottery which are in Mr. Boynton's Collection. This jug was made in two sizes. On either side of the larger ones is the figure of an uncouth and slovenly looking man in red coat, pink waistcoat, striped green and white under-waistcoat, orange necker-chief, orange breeches above which his shirt is seen, top boots and spurs. In his hand he holds his hat, orange with red ribbons, on which is a card bearing the words. " Milton for ever." Beneath the spout on a scroll is the following curious verse :—

> " The Figure there is no mistaking,
> It is the famous Man for—*breaking*,
> Oh that instead of Horse and Mare
> He had but broken Crockery-ware,
> Each grateful Potter in a bumper
> Might drink the health of
> Orange Jumper."

The history of this man is so interesting that I here quote Jewitt's account of him verbatim.

" This man who was known all the country round as ' Orange Jumper,' was a very eccentric character, and a great mover in the political ' stirs' of his county. He was a horse breaker at Went-worth, and many extraordinary stories are remembered in connec-tion with him. One of these as connected with the story of this jug is worth repeating. In the great Yorkshire election of 1807— the most costly and the most strongly contested election on record —when the candidates who were so mercilessly pitted against each other were Lord Milton, Wilberforce, and Lascelles, ' Orange Jumper' was employed to carry dispatches regularly backwards and forwards from York to Wentworth House, the seat of Earl Fitzwilliam, the father of Lord Milton, who eventually won the election, and was returned as the colleague of Wilberforce. Orange was the Fitzwilliam colour, and blue that of Lascelles (son of the Earl of Harewood) his opponent ; and on one occasion ' Jumper' was seen entering York decked out as usual in orange, but riding on an ass gaily decorated with bright blue ribands. On being jeered at for this apparent inconsistency in wearing both colours, he replied that *he* wore the right colour, orange, and that his ass was only like other asses, for they were all donkeys that wore blue ! "

Fig. 12. FRUIT DISH. Mr. O. Grabham's Collection.

Fig. 13. PLATE. York Museum Collection.

The election was gained by the party he espoused, and in commemoration these jugs, with his portrait and verse, were made. They are marked

DON POTTERY

pencilled in red on the bottom.

On the quart jugs the figure appeared on one side, and the verse on the other.

Fig. 14. The Jumper Jug. Mr. T. Boynton's Collection.

An engraved pattern book was issued by the firm, in the same style, and of the same size as that of Hartley, Greens and Co., of the Leeds Pottery, many of the Don patterns are identical with those of Leeds. A careful comparison of the two books reveals the fact that whereas in the latest edition of that of Leeds 269 patterns are engraved, in that of the Don Pottery 292 are given.

I have in my possession a very pretty dessert service of fine Don earthenware, the comport dishes and plates being each of them ornamented inside, with a different flower, stem, and leaves, beautifully painted, and on the back the name of the same printed in red.

Mr. Hurst has some fine pieces, and the same may be said of our own Collection.

About 1810—12, China of an excellent quality was, according to Jewitt, made at the Don Pottery, to a very small extent. These are so rare that I have neither seen a piece myself, nor have I come across any one else who has been fortunate enough to do so.

Fig. 15.  Tea Service.  Mr. A. Hurst's and Mr. O. Grabham's Collection.

The marks used at this pottery were
DON POTTERY pencilled in red on the bottom of the vessel.
DON POTTERY impressed on the bottom of the pieces.
    GREEN
DON POTTERY also impressed
GREEN DON POTTERY printed and transferred in blue, round the demi-lion rampant also in blue, on the bottom of the vessels.

The demi-lion rampant holding in his paws a pennon with DON upon it and POTTERY below, either all impressed or all printed and transferred in blue.  Fig. 16, *a*.

*a*          Fig. 16.          *b*

After Samuel Barker purchased the Don Pottery in 1834, the demi-lion holding the pennon, a little altered in shape and mane, was still used.  Above the pennon was sometimes BARKER, sometimes B. and sometimes nothing, whilst on the pennon was DON, and POTTERY below, all printed and transferred in blue.  Fig. 16, *b*.

The next two marks were adopted by the firm after it had become Samuel Barker and Son in 1851, namely, an Eagle displayed rising out of a ducal coronet, and the demi-lion rampant holding in his paws the pennon enclosed within a garter, beneath which are the initials of the firm S. B. & S. both in blue transfer. Fig. 17.

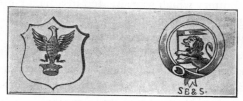

Fig. 17.

## ECCLESHILL POTTERY.

Situated near Bradford, the Manor House Potteries at Eccleshill were established about the year 1835, and were carried on as a manufactory of stoneware until the year 1867 under the proprietorship of a Mr. Woodhead, whose object was to utilize the bed of fireclay found in the locality. The venture had not, unfortunately, the success which it deserved. Much of the pottery made is of exceptionally good design and quality, and compares quite favourably with the celebrated Nottingham and Brampton stonewares, with which it is frequently confused, as no distinguishing mark was used at Eccleshill.

Articles of great variety were made, consisting of household utensils, ornaments, garden vases, etc., as well as busts and statuettes of celebrated people of the early 19th century, viz. : Nelson, Wellington, Burns, Byron, Scott and others, these ranging in size from a few inches to several feet ; jugs, cradles, knife-boxes, salt-kits, etc., were also made here, and puzzle jugs with raised figures round the belly.

Mr. Herbert Maltby, curator of the Bolling Hall Museum, Bradford, to whom I am indebted for most of the above information, tells me that all the objects were salt-glazed, and of brown stoneware. In common with all the other neighbouring potteries at Howcans, Denholme, Thornton, Elland, etc., the trade was eventually killed by the markets being supplied by a better and cheaper ware from Staffordshire.

There are several fine pieces of Eccleshill ware in the Bolling Hall Museum.

# FALSGRAVE POTTERY.

A suburb of Scarborough. It is stated in " Memorials of Scarborough," by C. Meadley, published in 1890, that " during the close of the 18th and the first part of the 19th century, Falsgrave boasted of a pottery which was situated in a field close to the then Horse Pond, and near the first milestone from Scarborough in ' Gallows Close ' where the North Eastern Railway now has its goods depot. The parties who carried on the establishment lived in a thatched cottage, and it formed the last house in the first row of houses as you entered Falsgrave from Scarborough. Either from the badness of the material, or from want of artistic skill, the productions of the pottery were so humble that it became a proverbial saying, when anything of a low character presented itself, ' that it was like Falsgrave China, rough and ugly,—as coarse as Falsgrave pottery.' "

However this may be, there is in the Scarborough Museum a very fair light brown bowl banded with blue, made at the Falsgrave Pottery. Mr. W. J. Clarke, of Scarborough, tells me that this bowl was presented to the Scarborough Museum by Mrs. Skeet (née Lacy, an old Scarborough family), and that according to the late James Chapman, of Scarborough, who died at an advanced age, the pottery was manufactured on the site where the North Eastern Railway goods station now stands, in the latter part of the 18th century. The clay for the same was brought from what is now Malton's Brick Yard on the Scalby road.

In connection with Scarborough—although in this paper I am not dealing with mediæval potteries—I should just like to mention a large one which was there in mediæval times, situated outside the boundary of the town. Mr. J. H. Hargreaves, of Scarborough, tells me that it was either on the site near the Roman Catholic church, on the ground now occupied by Wilson's Free Dwellings, or on that where Chapman's Boarding House is situated. From the Museum reports at Scarborough it seems that there must have been a very extensive manufactory. Green glazed pottery is occasionally found a few inches below the surface of the ground.

In 1854, excavations brought to light a long series of arches forming what had evidently been the kilns of the pottery. The structure of the bricks of which they were composed being assigned by competent judges to belong to the 14th century. Two of these arches were carefully dug out and transported to the Museum, at

Mr. Nesfield's expense. The works seem to have extended from New Queen Street to Mulgrave Terrace. They must often have been seriously interrupted, and probably owe their ultimate extinction to this inconvenient proximity to such scenes of strife as those enacted round the castle.

In the Scarborough Museum is an Aquamanile, a curious very early vessel, which was doubtless made there. It is in the form of an animal, most probably a ram, with a twisted horn, but unfortunately its handle and other parts are imperfect. It is covered with a rich green glaze. Fragments of similar vessels have been found in York, and are in our Collection.

Fig. 18. Bowl. Scarborough Museum Collection.

## FERRYBRIDGE & KNOTTINGLEY POTTERY.

Thoresby records that Francis Place, of the Manor House at York, spent much money upon his manufacture of " fine muggs," and that he attempted it solely from a turn for experiments ; but one Clifton, of Pontefract, took the hint from him, and made a fortune by it.

The works of Clifton would probably be the forerunners of those at Ferrybridge, near the town of liquorice, so famous for its " Pomfret cakes."

The pot works at Ferrybridge are amongst the largest in Yorkshire. They were established in 1792 by Mr. William Tomlinson, whose partners were Mr. Seaton, banker, of Pontefract ; Mr. Foster, ship-owner, of Selby ; Mr. Timothy Smith, a coal proprietor ; and Mr. Thompson, of independent means, of Selby.

The firm was styled " William Tomlinson and Co." until about
the year 1796, when the proprietors took into partnership Ralph
Wedgwood, of Burslem, when the style was changed to that of
" Tomlinson, Foster, Wedgwood, and Co." Ralph Wedgwood
was a nephew of the great Josiah.   He was a man of considerable
inventive genius, but too eccentric and visionary for the affairs of
every-day life, and in consequence of the great expense involved
in following out his experiments, the partnership was dissolved in
1800 or 1801, and the style " Tomlinson and Co." was resumed,
and so continued until 1834, when it was changed to " Tomlinson,
Plowes, and Co.," Mr. Plowes of the Castleford Pottery having
joined the proprietary.

In 1804 the name of the manufactory, which up to that period
had been called the Knottingley Pottery, was changed to that of
the Ferrybridge Pottery.  This change was made for the con-
venience of foreign correspondence, a large foreign trade being
carried on, Ferrybridge being at that time a post town of some
note, and the works being situated nearer to it than Knottingley.

Mr. Tomlinson was succeeded by his son Edward Tomlinson,
who continued the works under the firm of " Edward Tomlinson
and Co." until the year 1826, when he finally retired.  A part
of the premises was then worked for a short time by Messrs.
Wigglesworth and Ingham, when the whole place was taken by
Messrs. Reed, Taylor, and Kelsall, who continued the manufactory
until the retirement of Mr. Kelsall, after which the works were
continued by the surviving partners, Messrs. James Reed and
Benjamin Taylor.  Mr. Reed, who was father of John Reed, of
the Mexborough Pottery, was a man of great practical skill, and
in his time many improvements in the ware were made and the
manufacture of China introduced, but only for a short period.  He,
in conjunction with his partners, took the Mexborough Pottery,
and for some time carried on the two establishments conjointly.
Ultimately Mr. Reed gave up the Ferrybridge works, and confined
himself to those of Mexborough, whilst Mr. Taylor carried on the
Ferrybridge works alone.

After Mr. Taylor gave up the works, Mr. Lewis Woolf entered
upon them as tenant for a few years, and in 1856 became the
purchaser and commenced manufacturing in his own name.  In
the following year, 1857, a large additional pottery was built
closely adjoining and connected with the Ferrybridge Pottery,
by the sons of Mr. Lewis Woolf.  This new manufactory was

called the "Australian Pottery." The proprietors of the joint works, the "Ferrybridge and Australian Potteries," were Lewis, Sidney, and Henry Woolf, who traded under the style of "Lewis Woolf and Sons." Sidney Woolf, the head of the firm was M.P. for Pontefract from 1880 to 1885. In 1873, the Rock Pottery, Mexborough, was purchased by Messrs. Sidney Woolf and Co.. but in 1883 they came to grief and severed their connection both with the Ferrybridge and the Mexborough Pottery.

Ferrybridge still continues to make a good deal of pottery. A group of three potteries lie all together on the west side of the road to Knottingley. The first of the group is the West Riding Pottery, founded about thirty years ago by Poulson Brothers, who employ 300 hands, of whom more than 100 are women. They make no brown ware, only printed ware. The same firm once carried on the original Ferrybridge Pottery, which is now in the hands of Messrs. Sefton and Brown, but the pottery as it was worked by Lewis Woolf is now divided into two parts, the Australian Pottery—the one built about 1857 by Mr. Woolf for his sons— being now carried on by Mr. Joseph Horn.

These works besides a very large local and coasting trade, had extensive transactions with several foreign ports, and from their first establishment to the time of the issuing of the famous Berlin decree by Napoleon, did a large and lucrative trade with Russia. The decree cut short the trade with the continent, a blow which was severely felt by the Yorkshire potters, but shortly afterwards, when the River Plate was opened up, one of the partners proceeded there and opened an establishment, and afterwards went on to Rio de Janeiro.

The wares principally produced were cream and cane-coloured, green-glazed ware, black basalt or Egyptian ware, printed ware, etc.

Marked examples are by no means common, though a fair number are to be found in public and private collections. We have a fine series, and so has Mr. Hurst.

Three interesting pieces in our Collection are a teapot and sugar basin in cane coloured ware, both having a blue medallion on each side containing the profile of a head in black, made in Ralph Wedgwood's time, and marked impressed on the bottom,

### WEDGWOOD & Co.

and a white plate with the "grass edge" pattern in dark blue all

c

round it, and in the centre a loaded pack-horse in dark blue with
a W on the blinker, the W standing for Wedgwood, when Ralph
Wedgwood was a member of the firm.  This was kindly presented
to us by Mr. J. R. Triffitt.

I possess a fine large jug, white, with green lines, a face or mask
for a spout, on one side a very clear cut bust of Lord Byron ! and
on the other a nude lady mounted bareback upon a horse, about
to drive a spear into a lion which has its claws fastened in the
horse's neck ; also some fine rich blue plates with the " willow
pattern " upon them, formerly belonging to old Mark Lightowler,
who kept the toll bar between Pontefract and Carleton, when I
was a boy.

The marks used at Ferrybridge were

TOMLINSON & CO. impressed on the bottom of the ware.

WEDGWOOD & CO. during the time of Ralph Wedgwood's
connection with the works, also impressed.

FERRYBRIDGE, impressed, and one variety of which mark
is peculiar from having the letter D reversed thus ꓷ

FERRYBRIꓷGE,

a shield with the words opaque granite China in three lines
supported by a lion and unicorn, and surmounted by a crown,
impressed in the ware.

Later—the lion and unicorn with the shield and crown, and the
words, " Ferrybridge and Australian Potteries," sometimes impressed and at others printed on the goods, with the names of the
bodies, as " granite," " stone-china," etc., added.

As before mentioned up to the year 1804, the manufactory was
known as the Knottingley Pottery, and a special brown ware was
made there.

The punch bowls, made for the cock-pits, with fighting cocks
and foliage upon them, done in " sgraffito," scratched ware,
specimens of which are in our Collection and in the Pontefract
Museum, were made at the Knottingley Pottery.

A man named Masterman used to have a small kiln in " The
Holes," Knottingley, where he made small pot figures as mantel-
piece ornaments, toys, etc., and sold them on a stall in Pontefract
market every Saturday, when I was a boy.

We have a very crude but very interesting figure of Little Red
Riding Hood with the wolf in our Collection, made here by
Masterman.

Fig. 19.  TEAPOT.  York Museum Collection.

Fig. 20.  JUG.  Mr. O. Grabham's Collection.

Fig. 21.  PLATE.  York Museum Collection.

Fig. 22.  PONTEFRACT CASTLE WATCH STAND.  York Museum Collection.

Fig. 23. WOLF AND RED RIDING HOOD. *Circa.* 1870. York Museum Collection.

OLD KNOTTINGLEY POTTERY.

Fig. 24. PUNCH BOWL. York Museum Collection.

# HOWCANS or POT HOWCANS POTTERY.

Near Ovenden, Halifax, a pottery was started here somewhere
about the middle of the 17th century, and slip ware and black
glazed articles of various kinds were made by a family of the name
of Halliday.   Mr. Nicholas Taylor, late of the Denholme Pottery,
to whom I am indebted for much information about these South
Yorkshire Potteries, says that the Hallidays first started as potters
at Puel Nick, about 1½ miles from Halifax, and there is still the
name of Potters Yard at Puel.   From here they established them-
selves at Bateain, about 2½ miles from Halifax, and half-a-mile
beyond Howcans.   Bateain farm was in the tenancy of Hallidays
from about 1655 to 1872, Tom Halliday giving up the farm in
1872, but the pottery at Puel was closed many years before this.
The estate belonged to the family of Deardings.   The business
was removed to Howcans and was carried on there for over a
hundred years, the works being finally closed in 1889, still under
the Hallidays.

Mr. Taylor worked at the Howcans Pottery for some time, and
he has in his possession a most interesting indenture, dated 1789,
which he obtained from one of the Hallidays.   The indenture was
in regard to this man's grandfather being apprenticed to pot
making.

Potting at Howcans and at Bateain must have been carried on
very largely, for in scarcely any part of the estate can excavations
be made without potsherds in plenty being turned up.

As at all these South Yorkshire Potteries, black ware and red
ware, ornamented with a bright dark brown glaze and a yellow
slip were made, the ornamentation in slip being done by inlaying,
relief, or quill stringing.   Many prints in relief were done at
Howcans.   Tea caddies, knife boxes, cradles, teapots, tobacco-
boxes, ornamental flower pots, puzzle jugs, salt kits, money boxes,
etc., were made here.   A fine series is contained in the Bankfield
Museum, Halifax, collected by Mr. Ling Roth.   We have several
specimens, also some fragments of a very beautiful marbled and
combed ware, made here.

Fig. 25. KNIFE BOX. York Museum Collection.

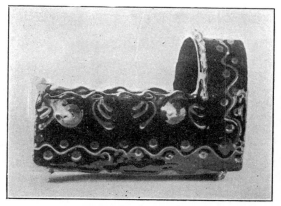

Fig. 26. CRADLE, date 1802. York Museum Collection.

Fig. 27. HEN AND CHICKENS MONEY BOX
IN "SNAIL HORN" WARE. York Museum Coll.

Fig. 28. SALT KIT.
York Museum Collection.

# HUDDERSFIELD.

## LINDLEY MOOR POTTERIES, Salendine Nook,

More than three hundred years ago, about the time of the accession of Queen Elizabeth to the throne of England, a numerous Scotch family of the name of Morton fled from Scotland to escape the persecution then raging against the Protestant religion in that country. They were potters by trade, and settled at Salendine Nook, in the parish of Huddersfield. They brought some workmen with them, and fetched others out of Staffordshire, and started a pottery business at Nook, which has been carried on in the district to this day.

Two district firms of the name of Morton are still carrying on business.

Some of the Mortons started a pottery at Hexley about 1868. Shortly afterwards they went to Siddall, near Halifax, but soon gave up. Some of the Hallidays from the Howcans Pottery then took it, but after a couple of years they failed, and it was finally closed down about 1870. Chiefly black ware was made there.

The Mortons, fire brick manufacturers at Siddall, are descendants of the original Mortons of Salendine Nook.

The potteries at Salendine Nook are carried on as Enos Morton and Sons, and Joseph Morton and Sons. Brown and red ware are made.

# HULL POTTERY.

Pot works are said to have existed at Hull in the middle of the 17th century. Land at Sculcoates, formerly an outskirt of Hull, has always been known by the name of "Pot House Yard." Clay pipe making was also carried on here.

In 1802, a plot of land on the Humber bank, in a part of what was then the outskirts of the town and known as "Myton," was sold by Thomas English, of Hull, to James Smith and Jeremiah Smith, both of Hull, potters; Job Ridgway, of Shelton, Staffordshire, potter; and Josiah Hipwood, of Hull, blockmaker. That part of the town for many years was known as the "Pottery" a name doubtless derived from these works. In 1806 the proprietors assigned all their interest in the works to Messrs. Job and George Ridgway, who carried them on for some years.

In 1826 Mr. William Bell became the proprietor of the works, and by him they were much extended, and operations were carried on on a large scale, chiefly for export, the principle part of the trade being with Hamburg, where his brother, Mr. Edward Bell was in business, and a large German and Dutch trade was done through his means.   The works were closed in 1841.

Fig. 29.   PLATE.   Hull Museum Collection.

A large variety of different kinds of ware were produced at Hull, and it is somewhat strange that marked pieces are so difficult to obtain.   One notable dinner service was made to commemorate an exploit in connection with the noted pirate, Paul Jones, and was made for the owner or family of the owner of the merchant ship, the " Crow Isle."   Only one plate of this service is now known to exist, and this is preserved in the Hull Museum, to which it was presented by the late Mr. Charles Hassell, grandson to the late Mr. Francis Hall, of Hull, who was the owner of the " Crow Isle," Baltic trader.

In the centre is represented the " Crow Isle " successfully beating off Paul Jones on its homeward voyage when off the Yorkshire coast in 1779.

Mr. Boynton has a very fine teapot ornamented in black transfer. The bell-shaped lid is said to be peculiar to these works.

In our Collection are two plates, one ornamented with the popular "willow" pattern in a rather peculiar but pretty shade of blue, whilst the other is of an unusual shade of yellow.

Fig. 30.   TEAPOT.   Mr. T. Boynton's Collection.

The marks are two bells, one generally overlapping the other, surrounded by the words, BELLE VUE POTTERY, HULL, in a circle, bells and letters all impressed in the ware, but sometimes the bells appear alone without the lettering, and in others the words Belle Vue Pottery, Hull, are in writing letters in blue, with scrolls and flourishes, surrounding the two bells also in blue.

Our willow pattern plate has both the impressed and the writing mark.

Fig. 31. PLATE. York Museum Collection.

Fig. 32. PLATE SHOWING IMPRFSSED AND PRINTED MARKS.
York Museum Collection.

# KILNHURST POTTERY.

A place which one would naturally say took its name from pot-works, Kilnhurst is situated mid·way between Doncaster and Sheffield, nine miles from each town. It is in the parish of Raw-marsh on the extreme boundary line, and adjoins the colliery village from which it takes its name. The works were first instituted in the year 1746, and the manufacture of earthenware has continued uninterruptedly to the present time. It can be claimed therefore, that it is the oldest established pottery business in Yorkshire. The works were started soon after the Act for the navigation of the river Don was obtained. They were erected on the estate of the Shore family, and held at the beginning of the 19th century by a potter named Hawley, who had a pottery at Rawmarsh.

From him it passed into the hands of George Green (one of the family of the Greens at Leeds) by whom on the 25th of April, 1832, it was purchased by Messrs. Brameld and Co. (subject to Mr. Shore, the owner, accepting them as tenants) at a valuation, Mr. Green to retain all the manufactured goods, copper plates, moulds, etc., and to reduce as much as convenient the stock of raw materials.

In 1839 it passed into the hands of " Twigg Brothers," who worked it conjointly with the Newhill Pottery after the death of their father, Joseph Twigg, who started the Newhill works in 1822. This Joseph Twigg was formerly employed as a working potter at the Rockingham Pottery, Swinton, before commencing for himself. His three sons, Joseph, John, and Benjamin, constituted the firm of Twigg Brothers. The two eldest, Joseph and John, were potters by trade, and, like their father, were employed at the " Rockingham Works." The youngest, Benjamin, was a joiner by trade.

The firm of " Twigg Brothers " continued until the year 1852, when Benjamin Twigg died. Joseph Twigg, the eldest brother having died previously, John Twigg thus became sole proprietor of the Kilnhurst Pottery, and remained so up to the date of his death on June 22nd, 1877. He was born on December 1st, 1801.

John Twigg had five sons, but with the exception of the youngest, Daniel, they all pre-deceased him, and the business was carried on by the said Daniel Twigg and under his own name to March 1884, when it was purchased by William Simpson Hepworth and his son-in-law, Bowman Heald, and has since been and is now carried on under the style of " Hepworth aud Heald."   The Mr. Hepworth mentioned was a printer and stationer, and for forty years he was postmaster at Knottingley.   He published several works, amongst them " The History and Antiquities of Knottingley," 1871, and the amusing " Life and Adventures of Jimmy Hurst of Rawcliffe." Mr. Hepworth died on November 14th, 1888, and Mr. Bowman Heald became sole proprietor of the works and continues as such at the present time.   Daniel Twigg, the last of the family connected with the trade, died on April 17th, 1892.

Fig. 33.   JUG WITH DRAGON HANDLE.   Mr. A. Hurst's Collection.

John Twigg produced most of the goods without any mark, but TWIGG was occasionally impressed on the bottom of the ware, or his initials J. T. were impressed or printed in blue transfer under the name of the pattern.

We have several pieces marked TWIGG, impressed, and Mr. Hurst has one marked TWIGG'S, a very fine jug after the style of the Mason jugs, with a dragon handle.

As regards the present period, Mr. Bowman Heald, to whom I am indebted for most of the information about this pottery, tells me that the goods produced are the usual useful domestic earthenware required by the middle and working classes, in printed, painted, sponged, banded, mosaic, etc., on white and ivory bodies, including dinner, tea, and toilet wares, etc.

When the works were taken over by Messrs. Hepworth and Heald, Mr. Bowman Heald introduced what is termed the "Bristol Ware," made in various sizes of mugs and jugs, such as are used in the Eastern counties and the South of England and in London. These goods were formerly made at one of the Bristol Potteries (since discontinued) exclusively, hence its name. Gradually Kilnhurst secured almost the whole trade in this particular line, and is now practically the only maker of these goods. One great advantage is that they are able to produce them with the guarantee that they are non-crazing. Within the twenty-three years from 1884 to 1907, over one million Bristol mugs and jugs were sold. This ware is of a dull cream colour with a broad hand of brownish-yellow on the top and on the top of the handle. Busts and foliage are moulded on to the sides of the body of the pieces.

Fig. 34. JUG. "BRISTOL WARE." York Museum Collection.

Besides the home trade a considerable export business is done, chiefly to Morocco, Australia, and the West Indian Settlements. Orders for Morocco have been executed continually and continuously for the past five-and-twenty years in spite of strong German competition.

Kilnhurst Pottery is splendidly situated as regards its position, being in the centre of the South Yorkshire coalfield, and adjoining Thrybergh Colliery with which it is connected by sidings, and having eight other large collieries within a radius of four miles. It is built close to the canal on which it has a wharf, and the Midland Railway Co's. main line, and the Great Central Railway Co. run on either side of it.

Kilnhurst possesses a fine series of models, collected from the "Rockingham," "Don," and "Mexborough" Potteries. Several examples of these have been reproduced from the original moulds, such as jugs, teapots, and cheese stands, and exhibit beautifully modelled work, especially those from the "Don" Pottery.

During the time the works have been in Mr. Bowman Heald's possession, several new features have been adopted in the mode of manufacture. The printing is now done by machinery on roller engravings, in place of the old system by flat copper plates, one machine turning out work equal to six men. Also the grinding of glaze and other materials has been economized by the introduction of Alsing's rotatory grinding cylinders, a great improvement on the old fixed pan grinding system.

John Twigg, so long connected with this pottery, deserves more than a passing notice. He was a decidedly eccentric personality, and was the dominating figure during the whole time he was associated with the history of the village and works. He was a keen, shrewd business man, and quite an institution in Kilnhurst. He was a rigid teetotaler and non-smoker, although he owned a public house (the Nag's Head) which was within two hundred yards of his residence. Many amusing stories are related of him by the old inhabitants.

Another pottery not mentioned by Jewitt was established in Kilnhurst about the beginning of the 19th century. The manufactured goods consisted of coarse brown ware made from native clay, it was not an extensive affair, and was closed in 1860, the last to work it being a potter of the name of Bedford. It lay between Swinton and Mr. Heald's pottery. The square of cottages which now cover the site is called "Pottery Yard."

# LEEDS POTTERY.

This was the most famous pottery in the County, and the almost forgotten works there turned out thousands of pieces of the highest excellency. There is no doubt that pottery has been made at Leeds, or its immediate vicinity from the earliest times. Geologically speaking, Leeds is most favourably situated for the production of, at least, coarse earthenware, as in several parts of the neighbourhood beds of clay are found particularly suitable for this purpose, which no doubt have been worked for this class of ware from British and Roman periods down to our own time, as pointed out by Messrs. Joseph R. and Frank Kidson, in their classic work, entitled, "Historical Notices of the Leeds Old Pottery, with a description of its Wares, together with brief accounts of contemporary potteries in the immediate vicinity, hitherto unnoticed."

The Wortley bed of clay is eminently adapted for making stoneware, and is now extensively used by several firms for fire bricks and sanitary ware. Ralph Thoresby, in his *Ducatus Leodiensis*, published in 1715, mentions that in his day it was employed for making tobacco pipes. The village of Potters Newton evidently takes its name from a colony of potters settled there in early times.

Of the exact date of the first establishment of the Leeds Pottery nothing definite is known, it is however certain that it was in existence about the middle of the 18th century, and at that time wares of no ordinary degree of excellence were produced. The works were situated in Jack Lane, close to the Leathley Lane Pottery.

The first proprietors of whom there appears to be any record were two brothers named Green, in 1760, and it is said that their earliest productions were in black ware. It was then carried on by Humble, Green and Co.

The Greens were a notable family in the annals of Yorkshire Potting, for we find members of it proprietors of, or partners in, several potteries in the south of the County, viz.: the Don Pottery, the Swinton Pottery, and the Kilnhurst Pottery.

In 1783 the firm was Hartley, Greens and Co., and they had so far advanced in their work and were so well known by that year, as to justify them in issuing an elaborate book of "designs" of some of the articles they were producing, printed in English,

French, and German. This volume is now of considerable rarity. In 1785 and 1786, fresh editions of the catalogue and book of plates were issued, and as stated by Llewellynn Jewitt in his excellent account of the Leeds Pottery in his " Ceramic Art of Great Britain," the works at this time had been considerably enlarged, and the wares made were exported in large quantities to Germany, Holland, France, Spain, and Russia. So great had the concern become five years later (1791) that the yearly balance then struck amounted to over £51,500. In 1794, another edition of the catalogue and pattern book was issued.

Fig. 35.  POT-POURRI OR COCKLE VASE.  Mr. T. Boynton's Collection.

In the year 1800, two fresh partners, Ebenezer Green and E. Parsons, were added to the firm, and on the death of Mr. Hartley in 1820, though still carried on as " Hartley, Greens and Co." or as " Greens, Hartley and Co.," other changes took place. These repeated changes, and the unpleasantness and disputes that arose in consequence, were no doubt most detrimental to the concern,

D

which was ultimately thrown into Chancery and a large portion of the stock sold off.

In 1825 the affair was got out of Chancery, and passed by purchase into the hands of Mr. Samuel Wainwright, one of the partners. Shortly after this Mr. Wainwright took other partners, and traded under the style of " Wainwright and Co." Samuel Wainwright died during the terrible cholera epidemic which raged in the district in 1834, and the trustees carried on the business under the style of " The Leeds Pottery Company," and employed Stephen Chappell, who had been head cashier under Wainwright and Co., as their sole manager.

Fig. 36.  CHESTNUT BASKET AND STAND.   York Museum Collection.

This arrangement continued until the year 1840, when the trustees transferred the whole concern to Chappell who obtained it on very advantageous terms. Shortly after this his brother James became a partner in the concern, the firm then consisting simply of " Stephen and James Chappell," who continued the works until 1847, when they became bankrupt. The pottery was then carried on for about three years for the benefit of the creditors by the assignees, under the management of Mr. Richard Britton, who had for some time held a confidential position with Mr. Chappell.

In 1850 Mr. Britton and a Mr. Samuel Warburton took the property off the creditors' hands, and carried on under the style of " Warburton and Britton " until the year 1863, when, on the death of Mr. Warburton, Mr. Richard Britton became sole proprietor of the works. On July 1st, 1872, he was joined in partnership by his two eldest sons, John Broadbent Britton and Alfred Britton, the firm being styled " Richard Britton and Sons."

After this disastrous history of change of ownership, loss of trade, and bankruptcy, the works were finally closed in 1878. After a period of disuse, the pottery was revived for a few years by Messrs. Taylor, who made ordinary domestic ware. It then fell into ruins, and at the present time, considering its past glories and renown, presents a sad spectacle, only a shed or two, and the remains of one or two kilns being left, of what was once one of the most famous potteries in the kingdom.

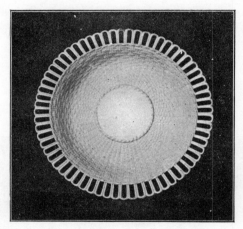

Fig. 37. PLATE WITH PERFORATIONS AND EMBOSSED BASKET WORK.
York Museum Collection.

In 1888, Mr. W. W. Slee, 30 Duncan Street, Leeds, revived the manufacture of the beautiful cream coloured ware, lustre ware, etc. He employed some of the workmen from the old works, and under his direction they turned out many capital pieces.

This pottery was only a small one, and was not on the old site, it is still in existence I believe.

In 1850, a man of the name of Yates, who had a china and earthenware shop in Leeds, had his ware marked "Yates, Leeds," but he neither made nor decorated the ware.

Fig. 38. MELON TUREEN AND LADLE. Mr. T. Boynton's Collection.

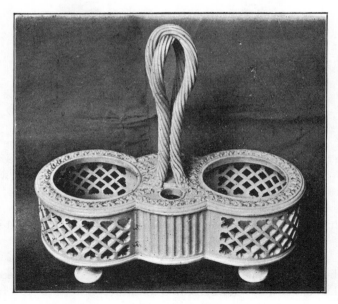

Fig. 39. CRUET STAND. York Museum Collection.

The wares manufactured at different periods at these most interesting works were :—

   1.   Coarse brown and red earthenware, some of it having a black glaze, made from the local clay on the first establishment of the pottery.

   2.   Delft ware, produced only in small quantities, and for a short period.

   3.   Hard and highly vitrified stoneware, with a strong salt glaze.

   4.   The famous cream or Queen's ware.

   5.   Black transfer printing on cream ware.

   6.   Ware decorated with colour.

   7.   Lustre, agate, and tortoise-shell wares.

   8.   Black Egyptian ware or black basaltes.

   9.   Blue printed ware.

   10,   Yellow ware, Rockingham ware, etc.

   11.   Figures, busts, etc.

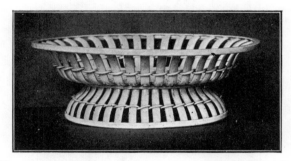

Fig. 40. DOUBLE TWIG BASKET. Mr. A. Hurst's Collection.

The famous Queen's, called after Queen Charlotte, or cream coloured ware was the speciality for which the Leeds works became universally famed, and in it they successfully competed with Wedgwood. It is this kind of ware which is known amongst collectors as " Leeds Ware."

In colour, the old Leeds Ware, *i.e.*, the cream coloured earthenware, is of a peculiarly rich tint, usually rather deeper in tone than Wedgwood's Queen's Ware, and of a slightly yellowish cast. It is very light in weight. The body is particularly fine and hard, and the glaze of extremely good quality. This glaze was produced with arsenic, and its use is said to have been so deleterious to the workmen, that they usually became hopelessly crippled after four or five years exposure to its effects. Wherever this glaze runs into crevices it assumes a peculiar greenish hue. The more modern ware lacks this green tinge, it is much heavier, and has quite a different character of body, which is appreciable to the touch, the glaze is more glassy, white, and thickly coated.

Fig. 41. Centre Piece or Epergne. York Museum Collection.

In this beautiful ware many and varied objects were made, such as large cisterns, magnificent centre-pieces (epergnes), some of these with perforated hanging baskets for sweetmeats, etc. ; chest-nut baskets, cockle bowls, butter dishes, cruet stands, candlesticks, twig fruit baskets in which the "twigs" or "withies" are really composed of clay in long or short strips as occasion required, and then twisted and formed into shape ; melon tureens, in the form of a melon resting on a leaf ; soup tureens, the handles being formed of twisted stalks with foliated terminations, and the knob of the lid representing a small melon or a pomegranate, the skin bursting and showing the seeds, after an Oriental design ; quintal flower holders, wine coolers, dessert services, punch bowls and ladles, and scores of other beautiful things. The perforations, diamond and heart-shaped piercing, so characteristic of Leeds Ware, were done by means of a single hand punch, which the workman pressed against the soft clay, and not by a set of punches fixed in a machine as is often supposed.

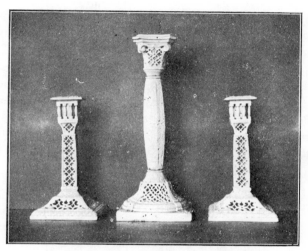

Fig. 42. OLD LEEDS CANDLESTICK in centre, York Museum Collection. The other two, Mr. Slee's make, Mr. O. Grabham's Collection.

A characteristic variety of Leeds work was the combination in basket work, etc., of embossed patterns with perforations, the actual centre of the plate or dish being left plain.

Jewitt states that the wholesale price of one of the magnificent chestnut baskets and stands probably produced about 1782—83, was, in 1794, 8s. 6d.—a price which collectors at the present time would gladly triple, and even quadruple. Dishes and plates were often decorated with the so-called "feather edge."

Many fine pieces of black printed ware were produced, such as plates with exotic birds, mugs and jugs with masonic emblems on them, also "Faith," "Hope," and "Charity" ; teapots bearing a transfer print of a medallion portrait of John Wesley, etc.

We have in our Collection two plates which commemorate the coronation of George IV. in reddish black transfer. The design is a crown in a garland, surrounded by the Rose, Shamrock, and Thistle, and on the garland

GEORGE IV CROWN'D July th19, 1821.

Painted ware. Many of these are quite excellent, whilst others are just as poor. A magnificent pair of vases or pot-pourri jars are in Mr. T. Boynton's Collection. They are about 12 inches high, with dark rich blue and gold body, having panels of well-painted groups of fruit and flowers. These were made by Messrs. Warburton and Britton about 1857. Amongst many other painted articles fine "rhytons" or drinking cups in the form of fox's masks and dog's heads were made.

A very rare ware made at Leeds was the so-called " Batavian " ware. These pieces are white inside, having a rich chocolate coloured glaze on the outside, except where shaped panels were left. The panels are decorated with imitations of Oriental decorations in blue under glaze colour. Mr. A. Hurst has a fine bowl in this ware, also a cream jug, having the usual Leeds twisted handle with foliated terminations.

Fig. 43.  JUG AND BOWL OF BATAVIAN WARE.  Mr. A. Hurst's Collection.

Towards the close of the 17th century, china ware, though costly, was imported both into England and the continent by means of the various East India Companies' ships. The Dutch, who possessed much of the Chinese trade, had a settlement called Batavia on the island of Java, and this served as a store for all kinds of Oriental goods collected by the Dutch traders from China, India, and other eastern countries, including a small portion from the, then, little known country of Japan.

The Batavian ware was so called from the belief that it was produced in the settlement of Batavia, but it really was an import from China or Japan.

In lustre ware some very fine pieces were made in the silver, copper, and purple or rose coloured lustre. The silver lustre was made largely for those who were unable to afford silver or Sheffield plate, and as existing types of plate were used as models, some excellent designs were turned out. We have in our Collection a beautiful little salt cellar in the rose coloured lustre.

Many mugs, jugs, tumblers, goblets. etc., were made in the agate and tortoise-shell ware, marbled, splashed, and mottled ; the decoration in these pieces being applied in the form of slip— not made up of a variety of coloured clays mingled together, as Whieldon and others did—and the slip is often worked up with a comb, feather, brush, or sponge on the Leeds pieces.

The black ware, also called black Egyptian and black basaltes or basalt, was made to a considerable extent about the year 1800 at the Leeds works. It is said to have a more decided bluish cast than is usual in other makes, and was almost entirely used for tea and coffee services, which were in great request at funeral parties. I have seen a few small ovals in this ware with busts of various celebrities in relief upon them, but I do not believe that any of these were made at the old Leeds works, and are very much more modern,

In the blue printed ware many patterns were used, and amongst them the " willow " and its variations. The early blue printed ware was of a peculiar rich strong blue, known as the Old Leeds Blue.

A canary yellow ware was made at Leeds. This is of considerable beauty, and is sometimes quite plain, whilst in other cases the pieces are decorated with vine leaves, tendrils. and grapes, in dark red. We have in our Collection a fine coffee pot with lid of the former, and a cup and saucer of the latter.

Several different jugs were made at Leeds. One of the most famous, of which a specimen is in the Collection of Mr. T. Boynton, is the rare "Vicar and Moses" jug, having on one side a spirited engraving of the Vicar and Moses, in black transfer: Moses with a lantern helping the Vicar, who is evidently half seas over, home; for these were the days when not only many of the laymen, but also considerable numbers of the clergy, seldom thought of going to bed before they had drunk at least two or three bottles of good old port. In front of the jug, pendant from the spout, is painted the arms of the borough of Leeds, the golden fleece, commonly called the "tup in trouble" with the initials J.B., beneath are the words, "Success to Leeds Manufactory," and on the other side the old ballad of the "Vicar and Moses" engraved in two columns, and surrounded by a border.

The first verse of the said ballad runs as follows :—

> "At the sign of the Horse, old Spin-text of course
> Each night took his pipe and his pot,
> O'er a jorum of Nappy, quite pleasant and happy
> Was placed this canonical Sot.
> Tol de rol de rol ti dol ti dol."

Fig. 44. THE VICAR AND MOSES JUG.   Mr. T. Boynton's Collection.

Fig. 45. PUZZLE JUG. York Museum Collection.

Fig. 46. PUZZLE JUG. York Museum Collection.

The well known Puzzle jugs or Teasing pitchers were made in considerable variety at Leeds, some of them being of very elaborate design whilst others were much plainer. They were used regularly in public houses for the amusement of the customers and to the advantage of the publican, as being very tricky articles to drink out of, much ale would be spilled, and this would have to be paid for, as well as that which was drunk.

These jugs often had amusing inscriptions on them, such as

" Within this jug there is good liquor
T'is fit for Parson or for Vicar ;
But how to drink and not to spill
Will try the utmost of your skill."

A very fine blue printed puzzle jug in our Collection has on it

A + Trifle

Shews + Respect

E + S

1799

This, like many of the early pieces of Leeds which have been turned, bears a small deeply cut circle in the bottom, done by the action of the lathe. By some authorities this mark is thought to be very characteristic of Leeds ware.

Fig. 47.   THE AGRICULTURAL JUG.   York Museum Collection.

The Agricultural jug, ornamented with various implements connected with agriculture, etc., was also popular. The 18th and early 19th century farmer was evidently more contented with his lot than his 20th century successor.

The following inscription appears on a jug in our Collection :—

### INDUSTRY.

Let the wealthy and great
Roll in splendor and state
I envy them not I declare it
I eat my own lamb
My own chicken and ham
I shear my own fleece and I wear it
I have lawns I have bowers
I have fruits I have flowers
The lark is my morning alarmer
So jolly boys now
Here's God speed the plough
Long life and success to the farmer.

This piece is dated 1823.

The John Gilpin jug in green with well moulded figures upon it. John Gilpin galloping past the "Bell" at Edmonton, with his wig flying behind him, etc.

Fig. 48. THE JOHN GILPIN JUG.    Fig. 49. THE AIRE JUG.

Mr. A. Hurst's Collection.

Fig. 50. THE NELSON JUG.       Fig. 51. THE NELSON JUG.

York Museum Collection.

Fig. 52. TOBY JUG.       Fig. 53. THE LORD MACAULAY JUG.

York Museum Collection.       Mr. G. Hill's Collection.

The Lord Nelson jug with a bust of the hero on one side, and a picture of the "Victory" in full sail on the other, on the front the Admiral's various titles.

The famous Toby jugs were also made at Leeds, as they were at many other potteries, representing a stout, fat-legged, jovial old fellow, bearing in one hand resting upon his knee, a jug or pot of foaming ale, and in the other a long clay pipe.

Mr. Hurst has a jug finely painted with bright plumaged birds, the spout of which represents the face and neck of the god or deity of the river Aire.

Electioneering, masonic, and many other jugs were made as well. Mr. George Hill, of Thornton Dale, has a very fine Lord Macaulay jug.

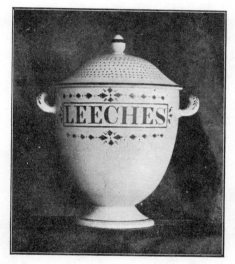

Fig. 54. LEECH JAR. Dr. J. L. Kirk's Collection.

A fine leech jar is in the possession of Dr. J. L. Kirk, Hungate Hall, Pickering. It is in cream ware, ornamented with dark red, two handles and perforated cover. Height 11 inches, with the word LEECHES upon it. Apothecaries' jars or drug pots were also made here.

Mr. Hurst has the centre part of a jelly mould, well painted with various fruits on either side, so that when brought on to the table in the midst of the clear transparent jelly the decorations would show through.

Fig. 55.  JELLY MOULD.  Mr. A. Hurst's Collection.

Many interesting mugs were made.

The Rodney mug: this is of large size, made to represent the head, face and neck, with the wig curls and hat of the famous Admiral Lord Rodney.

The Toad, Frog, and Lizard two-handled mugs were made having at the bottom, or crawling along the sides, a representation, well modelled and coloured, of one or two of the above reptiles; as the ale which covered them was drunk, the reptiles became

Fig. 56.  THE RODNEY MUG.         Fig. 57.  LIZARD AND FROG MUG.

Mr. A. Hurst's Collection.

visible, and were supposed to considerably astonish the drinker. Mr. Hurst has one which contains a lizard and two frogs.

In Mr. Wilson's Collection is a mug ornamented with lustre, on which is the following most pertinent advice to convivial spirits :—

> " Come my old friend and take a Pot
> But mark now what I say
> While that thou drinkst thy neighbour's health
> Drink not thine own away.
> It but too often is the case
> While we sit o'er a Pot
> We kindly wish our friends good Health
> Our own is quite forgot."

Fig. 58. FOX MASK SAUCE BOAT WITH SWAN HANDLE AND SWAN STAND.
York Museum Collection.

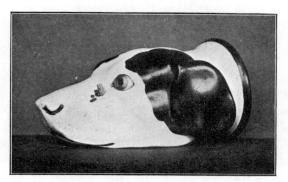

Fig. 59. HOUND'S HEAD RHYTON OR DRINKING CUP.
York Museum Collection

E

Electioneering and masonic mugs were made, as well as many others. Beautiful sauce boats in the shape of swans, fox's masks, fish, etc., were turned out, also cream jugs in the shape of cows, some with maids milking and some without. Jardinières of cornucopia form, elaborate tobacco pipes with the stem in several close round coils, fine tea-poys or tea-caddies, money boxes in the shape of plain and elaborate little cottages, and a thousand other articles quite beyond the scope of this paper to mention, much less to describe.

Finely modelled and coloured figures such as those in Mr. Hurst's Collection, representing " Neptune " and " Charity " were produced.

In the summer of 1781, busts of John Wesley were exhibited at the Methodist Conference in Leeds. These were most probably

Fig. 60. BUST OF JOHN WESLEY. Mr. J. R. Triffitt's Collection.

copied from that modelled by Enoch Wood, of Burslem, in that year. The teachings of John Wesley had gained many adherents in Yorkshire, and the Leeds Pottery is said to have done a great trade in jugs, having upon them a black transfer print of the preacher, and as before mentioned, teapots having the same design were largely manufactured.

A large figure of a horse with L.P. (Leeds Pottery) on one corner of the horse-cloth was made at an early date, and used by

Fig. 61. CHARITY AND NEPTUNE. Mr. A. Hurst's Collection.

Fig. 62. HORSE. York Museum Collection.

druggists and others as a sign that horse and cattle medicines were sold by them, in the same way that one made of plaster of Paris is now employed. Veterinary surgeons and saddlers also used them.

Fig. 63.  SALT CELLAR IN ROSE LUSTRE.  York Museum Collection.

Fig. 64.  BEAR.  Mr. J. R. Triffitt's Collection.

After much research on the matter, I have no doubt that many of the bear's grease pots, with finely painted lids representing bears, brown, black, and white, under various conditions, were produced at Leeds, though I have never been fortunate enough to meet with a marked specimen. Some of these represent a bear climbing up a pole in the Zoological gardens, the bear pit being surrounded by an admiring crowd ; soldiers shooting bears in the mountains, an old bear teaching the young bears their lessons, hunters chasing polar bears on ice, etc.

Mr. Triffitt has a very fine large figure of a polar bear standing on an ice floe, in Leeds ware, and on it in black letters,

## "GENUINE BEAR'S GREASE & COLD CREAM SOLD WITHIN."

Fig. 65.  BEAR'S GREASE POTS.  Mr. O. Grabham's Collection.

Fig. 66.  LIDS OF BEAR'S GREASE POTS.  Mr. O. Grabham's Collection.

To Messrs. R. Hendrie and Co., the well known perfumers and fancy soap makers, 4 Nile Street, City Road, London, N., I am indebted for the following advertisement, taken from the *Morning Herald* of May 31st, 1787, advertising a dead bear from which grease or fat could be obtained. I asked Messrs. Hendrie for what purpose the bear's grease was used, and they kindly replied as follows : " You ask for what purpose it is used. We can only make a guess, that because the bear is a hairy animal people think his fat must be good for producing hair ; but as to whether this has been put to any scientific test, we cannot say."

Fig. 67.  ADVERTISEMENT OF BEAR'S GREASE, "MORNING HERALD," MAY 31ST, 1787.

Fig. 68.  POT-POURRI JARS.  Mr. T. Boynton's Collection.

The marks adopted at the Leeds Pottery were

## LEEDS POTTERY *

in large capitals, with a terminal asterisk, impressed.

The same lettering, without the asterisk, in small capitals, impressed.

impressed in the form of a cross.

I have seen this twice repeated on a plate, forming a double cross, also with HARTLEY, GREENS & CO. in addition to the cross on another plate, all impressed

## HARTLEY, GREENS & CO.
## LEEDS * POTTERY

in a semi-circular form, impressed.

L.P. on the large figures of the horse, in black.

Leeds Pottery incised on the bottom of a goblet in writing letters.

LEEDS POTTERY in black transfer on the outside of a jug in the yellow ware, ornamented with grapes, leaves and tendrils in red.

R. B. & S. within an ornamental circle, which also gave the name of the pattern. This, according to Messrs. Kidson, for I have not seen a piece so marked myself, was printed in blue or other colours at the bottom of the plate or dish.

Another mark used by Mr. Britton is said by the same authorities to be the letter 𝔓 within a gothic quatrefoil in a circle, impressed.

The best Collection of Leeds ware that I have seen is undoubtedly that in the possession of Mr. Richard Wilson, Armley, Leeds. Mr. Thomas Boynton, Bridlington, has a very fine one, and so has Mr. Arthur Hurst, York, and my very best thanks are due to these gentlemen who have so kindly allowed me to examine most thoroughly the beautiful specimens in their possession.

We, also in the York Museum, have a fine series of Leeds Pottery.

Fig. 69.   Bowl with Perforated Outer Jacket.   York Museum Collection.

## LEEDS.
## HUNSLET HALL or PETTY'S POTTERY.

For the following account of this pottery, I am entirely indebted to Messrs. J. R. and F. Kidson, who give it in their classic work on "Leeds Pottery." The premises were still standing in 1892, in a ruinous condition, situated at the corner of Beeston Road and Holbeck Moor, but just within the township of Hunslet. After the Leeds Old Pottery it was in its day the most important of the Leeds local potteries. In 1792, the pottery was in the hands of Messrs Petty and Rainforth, but had been established some time.

They made cream and other wares of a similar type to that manufactured by Hartley, Greens and Co. Many of their productions were exported to Brazil. In 1817 to 1825, the firm was

Petty and Hewitt; from 1825 to 1845, it was styled Samuel Petty and Son. After this, Messrs. Petty, having by means of their exports to Brazil established a South American agency, retired from the earthenware business and went into another class of trade.

In 1847 the pottery passed into hands of Mr. John Mills, who had previously in conjunction with a Mr. Hepworth, worked the Leathley Lane factory. Mr. Mills held the concern for twenty or thirty years, when it finally passed into the hands of Taylor Brothers, who for some few years worked this, the old Pottery, and several others at the same time.

As far as is known no mark was used at this pottery, and pieces made here are very difficult to distinguish.

The other local potteries, which I have not space to more than mention, are dealt with by Messrs. Kidson in their " Leeds Old Pottery," and according to these authorities were: Taylor's Pottery, Allison's Pottery, Russell's Pottery, Marsden's Pottery, Leathley Lane Pottery, and Wibsey Pottery.

## LINTHORPE POTTERY.

When this pottery was given up in 1889, one of the most interesting of the industries in Middlesbrough came to an untimely end. It was established in 1879 by Mr. John Harrison, but owing to the sudden death of that gentleman, work ceased ten years later.

The site is now occupied by the Linthorpe Laundry, but originally it was the " Sun Brick Works," of which Mr. Harrison was the proprietor. In consequence of the suggestions of Dr. Dresser, the well-known architect and designer, who was struck with the suitability of the clay for the purpose, Mr. Harrison had some trial pieces made, with the result that he decided to lay down the necessary plant and commence the work of the potter. He was lucky in securing as his manager Mr. Henry Tooth, who afterwards went to the Bretby Art Pottery in Derbyshire, to whose skill and energy the success of the undertaking was very largely due.

During the early years of the manufactory the name of Chr. Dresser forms part of the impressed mark on the ware. A few early forms, including many of the No. 1 design —a small urn-shaped vase—lack even the impress LINTHORPE, but later the impress was LINTHORPE Chr. Dresser on the base of

all specimens, and this was followed by the word LINTHORPE
across an outline of the No. 1 design, with or without Dr. Dresser's
name, and very generally bearing in addition to the number of the
design the initials of Mr. Tooth, **H** or H. T.

At one time the works employed about one hundred hands, and
a very large amount of ware was turned out. Although at first
the forms of the productions were chiefly of the more severe and
classical type: Egyptian, Moorish, Indian, Chinese, Japanese,
Mexican, and Celtic designs were shortly attempted with great
success, and the delicate blendings of colours are much admired.

Fig. 70. VASE. York Museum Collection.

Every attention was paid to attaining to beauty of form, colouring
and glazing. The colours were subdued in tone, but included
many hues, though soft greens, greys, crimsons, and purples pre-
dominated. One peculiarity of the ware is that the brilliant
glazes often assumed an "accidental pattern," due to changes
which took place in the firing. As the proprietor stated in a

pamphlet, which is now somewhat scarce, "the Linthorpe Ware has been designed to meet a growing want of the present day; it will be found with its varied effects to accord with all the forms of art decoration, and to take its part in adding richness and beauty to an apartment without disturbing that general repose which we now seek to achieve in our rooms."

Vases, inkstands, etc., with flowers and leaves beautifully modelled in relief were made; and in the plain, richly-coloured glazes—rose bowls, tazzas, card trays, ewers, plaques, toilet ser-vices, ash trays, and many other useful and ornamental articles issued from the pottery, ranging in size from the tiny inch-high breakfast salt cellar to vases which counted their height in feet instead of inches.

Hearth and other tiles were also placed on the market, as well as a few samples of umbrella and walking-stick handles.

Fig. 71. VASE. Mr. O. Grabham's Collection.

A fine exhibition of Linthorpe Art Ware was held at the Dorman Memorial Museum, Middlesbrough, in 1906, for which a catalogue was compiled by Mr. Baker Hudson, the Curator, and it is from the excellent account of the Linthorpe Pottery here given that most of the above information is derived.

# MEXBOROUGH OLD POTTERY.

There were two well-known potteries situated here,, and marked pieces of the ware from either of them are decidedly rare.

The first was established at the end of the 18th century by Messrs. Sowter and Bromley, who held the works till 1804, when they came into the possession of Mr. Peter Barker, the son of Joseph Barker who came out of Staffordshire as manager of the Swinton works. He became partner with Mr. Wainwright at the pot works at Rawmarsh, afterwards Hawley's, and ultimately took to the works at Mexborough. These were continued by the brothers Peter and Jesse Barker, who were succeeded by Mr. Samuel Barker, the son of the latter, until the year 1834, when they acquired the Don Pottery. By Samuel Barker the works

Fig. 72. OVAL DISH WITH PERFORATIONS. York Museum Collections.

were continued until 1844, when they were discontinued, but the freehold was retained by the then owners, viz.: the Barker family, by whom it was converted into a foundry for the production of railway wagon wheels, etc. For many years it was carried on under the style of H. and S. Barker Ltd., but eventually was closed, and remained so for some years. Part of it in 1910 was being used as a foundry on a smaller scale than previously, and the other part as a glass bottle works. Very few people are aware that a pottery ever existed here, and I am indebted to Mr. Bowman Heald for the information. Its position was on the

canal side, about half way between the other Mexborough Pottery
and the Don Pottery.

The mark used, impressed in capitals in the ware, was

SOWTER & CO.
MEXBRO.

We have a teapot, in a pretty blue transfer, having a swan for a
knob on the top of the lid, also a well potted oval dish ornamented
with a variety of the popular "Willow" pattern in a pretty shade
of light blue and having large perforations along the outside.

# MEXBOROUGH.
## ROCK POTTERY or MEXBRO' POTTERY.

These works, at first very small, were established for the manufacture of brown and yellow wares and common red garden pots,
by a man named Beevers, who, with a partner named Ford, carried
on the business for some years. The workrooms at this time were
built close up to the natural rock, which indeed formed the back
wall of the pottery, and from this circumstance the place was
known as the "Rock Pottery."

The works next passed into the hands of Messrs. Reed and
Taylor, who owned the works at Ferrybridge.

In 1839 the pottery passed entirely into the hands of Mr. James
Reed, who carried it on till 1849, when he was succeeded by his
son Mr. John Reed, who altered the name from the "Rock" to
the "Mexbro'" Pottery, but amongst the inhabitants it always
was and is known as the "Rock Pottery." John Reed carried on
the work till his death in January, 1870, and his executors under
the management of Mr. C. Bullock till 1873, when it was purchased by Messrs. Sydney Woolf and Co., owners of the Old
Ferrybridge Pottery and of the Australian Pottery, Ferrybridge,
and managed by Mr. Bowman Heald, to whom I am indebted for
much information about this and other potteries in the district.

This firm worked the concern and did an extensive trade during
the following ten years, but at the end of 1883 their name dis-
appeared from the list of Yorkshire earthenware manufacturers,
and the two Ferrybridge Potteries passed into other hands. Mr.
Bowman Heald was manager here from 1873 to the time of the
closing down of the works in 1883.

The plant of the Rock Pottery, including engravings, moulds,
models, stock-in-trade, etc., were disposed of to a Swinton glass

bottle manufacturer, Mr. William Wilkinson, who after ten months trial relinquished the business, and finally he disposed of everything by auction, this being the finish of its history as a pottery.

The site being a valuable one, almost in the centre of Mexborough, the buildings and kilns were soon in the hands of the wreckers, and eventually a series of houses and shops, together with a handsome Wesleyan chapel, were erected on the spot, where for nearly a century the busy artisan had plied his craft. Prior to the sale Mr. Wilkinson allowed Mr. Bowman Heald to choose any models and designs that he cared to take, and he became the possessor of the model of the Keep of Conisborough Castle referred to by Jewitt, also of many other interesting models which formerly had been obtained at the dissolution of the old Rockingham and other works.

The marks used at the Rock Pottery were REED in large capitals impressed in the ware.

REED in blue letters printed on the bottom of a garland surmounted by a crown, the garland enclosing the words "stone ware," everything in blue. This is on a fine large jug or ewer in our Collection, printed in a deep rich blue with the same rural scene on each side, namely, a boy playing on Pan-pipes and some goats lying down.

Fig. 73.  LARGE EWER.  York Museum Collection.

## MIDDLESBROUGH POTTERY.

The Middlesbrough Pottery was established in 1834, when the population of the place was only about two hundred. It was the first of the public works, and was started by Richard Otley, Joseph Taylor, John Davison, Thomas Garbutt, and a few other local men, and at first made a better class earthenware chiefly for export. The first oven was fired in April 1834, and the first order shipped to Gibraltar in September of the same year. From 1834 to 1844 they traded as the Middlesbrough Pottery Co., and from the latter year to 1852 as the Middlesbrough Earthenware Co. From 1852 until the pottery was closed in 1887 the firm traded in the name of the proprietors, Messrs. Isaac Wilson and Co.

The early specimens of the ware bear the mark of the anchor, with or without the cable, with the words MIDDLESBRO POTTERY surrounding it in horse-shoe form, letters and anchor all impressed.

Fig. 74. MIDDLESBROUGH MARK.

Mr. Baker Hudson, the Museum, Middlesbrough, to whom I am indebted for most of this information, tells me that he had a talk with Mr. Lincoln, who for some thirty years was an employee of the firm, and according to the latter the firm had a warehouse and agent at Hamburg, and their trade there suffered a very definite eclipse when the Germans imposed a tariff upon English earthenware, whilst they could send their manufactures in here free. The same old story.

Two plates in the Dorman Memorial Museum, Middlesbrough, bear as a marking, an angel or well-grown cherub blowing a trumpet which bears a scroll on which appears the set or pattern number, and below this " I. W. & Co." beneath which, in horse-shoe form, MIDDLESBRO POTTERY appears in the same

Fig. 75. PLATE. Mr. O. Grabham's Collection.

Fig. 76. PLATE. Mr. O. Grabham's Collection.

Fig. 77. BOWL ORNAMENTED WITH LUSTRE. Mr. A. Hurst's Collection.

colour as the above transfers. Within the horse-shoe appears the anchor and over this a crown, both impressed in the ware. Mr. Lincoln says that the crown was used to mark the better class (white paste) ware, which they generally spoke of as "Crown Ware." These two plates of course belong to the Isaac Wilson and Co's. period.

I have seen several pieces impressed on the back

I. W. & Co. MIDDLESBRO.

and I have a plate with a view of some of the kilns of the pottery in brown transfer on the back.

Fig. 78. PLAQUE. York Museum Collection.

A curious mark on a plate in Mr. Hurst's Collection is LONDON in a semicircle, and below, the anchor and cable, all impressed in a kite-shaped form.

Chaffers, in his "Marks and Monograms on Pottery and Porcelain," 11th edition, 1906, gives a figure of the same mark with I S over the impress, and in this connection Mr. Baker Hudson tells me that there was a Mr. I. Sharpe connected with the early days of Middlesbrough, who also might have had something to do with the pottery, or the initials might stand for the London dealer who sold the ware.

F

# NAFFERTON POTTERY.

Miss Madeleine Longbottom, of Nethergate, Nafferton, tells me that the pottery was built in 1835, and bricks were being made there in 1844. The pot-kiln business was started in 1848 by one of Charles Longbottom's potters named Joseph Lagdon, who died in 1860.

Charles Longbottom started the pottery on October 6th, 1848, and it was closed down in Samuel Longbottom's time, April 27th, 1899.

There were three kilns: one for bricks and tiles, one for garden pots (a small one), and one for earthenware and glazed goods.

The Longbottoms bought a lot of glazed domestic ware from T. Hulme, Burslem, Staffordshire, and from others, and this being sold at the pottery made many people think that it was made there; but, with the exception of the white " biscuit " or unglazed pot-pourri vases with covers and handles, impressed underneath S. L. for Samuel Longbottom, the large two-handled ornamented vases, with covers, and certain flower stands and bowls nicely decorated with finely modelled and glazed ivy leaves and sprays upon them, mostly coarse rustic ware—garden chairs and seats—and garden pots were made here.

Fig. 79.  Pot-pourri Vase.  Mr. A. Hurst's Collection.

## NEWHILL POTTERY.

Situated near Wath-upon-Dearne, this pottery was established in 1822 by Mr. Joseph Twigg, who up to that time had the management of the Swinton Old Pottery, by whom, in partner- ship with his sons John, Benjamin, and Joseph Twigg, it was carried on until about 1866, when it passed into the hands of Messrs. Binney and Matthews, who were shortly afterwards succeeded by Messrs. Dibb and Coulter. In April, 1872, the works were purchased by Messrs. Bedford and Richmond, but were very soon closed down, and the site is now occupied by cottages.

Mr. Bowman Heald saw a quantity of white plates made here for export in 1871, but no mark was on them. But as marks are very rarely put upon any but printed ware this does not prove that the works had no mark. Although near the coal-field this pottery was badly situated, being some distance from the canal and railways which caused great expense in cartage, etc.

## RAWMARSH, near Rotherham, POTTERY.

William Hawley commenced potting about 1790, and carried on the manufacture of earthenware at the Top Pottery up to the time of his death in 1818, then in his 63rd year, after which the business was conducted by his wife Elizabeth, known as Dame Hawley, herself taking the active and important part of manage- ment, making domestic ware and tiles of a good quality for hearths, until she died in 1844 in her 85th year. The Dame was known for her shrewdness and general knowledge of pottery.

George, her son, now conducted the business, working it success- fully, and in a short time purchasing the Low Pottery, at Raw- marsh, which was previously carried on by Messrs. Taylor and Wainwright, and eventually closing down the Top Pottery. A few years afterwards the Low Pottery was purchased by a company, only to be carried on for a year or two, when it was bought back again into the Hawley family by Hawley Brothers, and carried on for the second time in conjunction with the Northfield Pottery, Rotherham. The Low Pottery was dismantled in 1905.

Another pottery, known as the Meadow Pottery, near Round- wood Brook, is said to have existed here, but I can obtain no information about it.

For much of this information, and for that concerning North- field Pottery, Rotherham, I am indebted to Mr. Sidney Hawley.

## ROCKINGHAM or SWINTON POTTERY.

At the beginning of the 18th century, a hard brown ware of much the same quality as that made at Nottingham and Chesterfield was produced on Swinton Common, where clays used for various purposes were abundantly found. In 1745, a Mr. Edward Butler established a tile yard and pot works for common earthenware on a part of the estate of Charles, Marquis of Rockingham, which lay close to Swinton Common. In 1765 the works were taken by William Malpass, who held another small pot work at Kilnhurst. With him were associated John Brameld and subsequently his son, William Brameld. In 1778 Mr. Thomas Bingley became a partner and the principal proprietor of the works at Swinton, and had for partners amongst others, John and William Brameld, and a man named Sharpe. The firm at this time was carried on under the style of " Thomas Bingley and Co." and did well.

From about the year 1787 down to 1800, the firm traded under the style of " Greens, Bingley and Co." This was owing to some of the Greens of the Leeds Pottery having become partners, and taken an active part in the Swinton manufactory with Bingley, Brameld, and those who were connected with them in these works.

Mr. John Green became acting manager of the Swinton works, and afterwards founded the Don Pottery. The partnership with John Green was carried on under the style of " Greens, Bingley and Co., Swinton Pottery," and the same price lists which were printed at Leeds, with the Leeds Pottery heading, had that heading cut off and that of Greens, Bingley and Co., Swinton Pottery," written in its place. Later on large fresh price lists were printed. They were headed " Greens, Hartley and Co., Swinton Pottery." The patterns used at Leeds were evidently to some extent adopted at Swinton. In 1796 the firm was " Greens, Bingley, and Co.," but was dissolved in 1806. At the dissolution of the partnership, the whole concern fell into the hands of two of the partners, Messrs. John and William Brameld who, with others, continued the works with considerable spirit under the style of " Brameld and Co." until their deaths. Additional buildings were erected, and cream coloured ware was made extensively, and the rare fine white earthenware, known as the " chalk body," which, owing to its costliness through loss in firing, was only made to a small extent.

In 1813 the sons of the old proprietors succeeded to the concern on the death of William Brameld, and many improvements were made. In 1825 the firm succumbed to the strain of financial difficulties, but Earl Fitzwilliam the owner of the property at Swinton came to the rescue, and the Swinton works were henceforth known as the Rockingham Works, and began to use the crest (a griffin) of the Fitzwilliam family as the mark of the firm. Although under the Bramelds the Rockingham works were eminently successful from an artistic point of view, they were not so commercially, and in 1842 were closed after involving not only their noble owner, but also the Bramelds in a loss of many thousands of pounds. The *chef-d'œuvre* of the Rockingham china works, the gorgeous dessert service made for William IV., for which £5,000 was paid, but which cost the producers considerably more, had much to do with the embarrassments that caused the final stoppage of the works.

After the stock was sold, Isaac Baguley, who was manager of the gilding department under the Bramelds, commenced business for himself on a small portion of the works by decorating and gilding goods purchased from other potteries. This he continued for eleven years to 1855, when his son, Alfred Baguley, succeeded him. Alfred Baguley continued the business on the old premises till the year 1865, when he removed to Mexborough and opened a china shop in High Street, about one hundred yards from the Mexborough Rock Pottery. In the yard at the rear of his house and shop he had a workshop and an enamelling kiln, in which he fired the finished goods after they had been decorated, etc. He carried on business here to the time of his death on March 7th, 1891. Neither of the Baguleys mentioned really manufactured any goods, they simply glazed and decorated them. Mr. Bowman Heald, of the Kilnhurst Pottery, tells me that he can speak from nearly twenty years knowledge of Mr. Alfred Baguley, as from 1872 to his death all his Rockingham ware was fired under Mr. Heald's direction at the "Mexborough Rock Pottery" and the Kilnhurst Pottery" respectively. He purchased the best Staffordshire china and earthenware in pure white from Minton's, Brown-Westhead, Moore and Co., and Powell, Bishop and Stonier; also at the Rock Pottery, Mexborough, Mr. Bowman Heald, from time to time made him quantities of jugs, coffee pots, beakers, etc., in white earthenware. All this ware, both china and earthenware, was in the "glost" finished state. Mr. A. Baguley never decorated

Fig. 80. FLINT MILL, ROCKINGHAM WORKS, 1908.

Fig. 81. OUTER SHELL OF KILN, ROCKINGHAM WORKS, 1908.

on the "biscuit" or unglazed ware, and it is very doubtful whether his father ever did so.

His process then was to " dip " or cover such parts as required with the original old Rockingham glaze, which he prepared and ground himself (the brown chocolate coloured glaze). The ware was then taken to one of the potteries mentioned, and fired in the ordinary manner in a " glost " kiln. Afterwards the gilding and decoration was done, also the printing from a copper-plate by transfer, by himself, of the mark, etc. Finally the ware was fixed in his "enamelling" kiln, which last process of course is necessary for all ware that is decorated and printed etc., *on* the glaze, not *under* it. It is termed the " hardening on " kiln.

Fig. 82.  Jug.                    Fig. 83.  Jug.

Mr. A. Hurst's Collection.

Alfred Baguley enjoyed the patronage of the Fitzwilliam family, and much of his Rockingham ware was produced for Wentworth House. His mark was the crest of Earl Fitzwilliam, viz.: a griffin and BAGULEY, ROCKINGHAM WORKS.

He was not allowed to use the crest except only for pieces that were made for the Fitzwilliam family. Others that he decorated, as for example a small chocolate pot in our Collection, of the old brown Rockingham glaze and gilded, were without the crest, and have ROCKINGHAM WORKS MEXBRO in a garland or garter running round BAGULEY in the middle, all printed in red.

Mr. Heald says: " I passed his little shop daily for many years, and remember his signboard in big letters,

A. Baguley, Rockingham Works.

On the death of Mr. Baguley the business was discontinued. He was quite an artist in his profession, and personally was a kind and genial man. He appreciated very much the privilege of fixing his ware as stated, for which firing only a nominal charge was made, and a few years before his death, he, wishing to tender an acknowledgment of my help—I hope I may put this without egotism—very kindly gave me the recipe for the old Rockingham glaze, as made by the Bramelds, and afterwards by his father and himself."

After the Rockingham works were closed in 1842, the flint mill in connection with the same was carried on for a year or two by one of the Brameld family, and later it came into the hands of James Parker, a former workman of Brameld's, by whom the flint grinding was continued till 1887, the ground flint being sold to different potteries in the district.

I. and I. Walker were the next to take over the flint mill business, but only had it for about twelve months, when they gave it up, and the works have remained entirely closed since then. A few years ago the engines, boilers, and flint milling machinery were demolished and sold as scrap iron.

The place, although situated in a beautifully wooded part of Swinton Common within three or four miles of Wentworth House, presents a ruinous, and considering its past renown, a sad spectacle. Whatever its position as a manufactory may have been considered in the past, it is now unsuitable for such a purpose, being quite isolated from the river and railways. One interesting remnant of the works is still in existence, this is the outer shell of one of the largest kilns, and is in a good state of preservation. It has been converted into a small pox isolation hospital, and was used as such some years ago. Plates of this and the flint mill, both of which I photographed in 1908, are reproduced.

James Montgomery the poet, and the Bramelds were great friends.

As before mentioned, up to the year 1825, the works were known as the Swinton Pottery, and after that date as the Rockingham

Works. Many beautiful and valuable pieces were made here both in earthenware and in porcelain.

The famous "Brown China" or Rockingham Ware which has been copied, but never quite successfully, by almost every manufactory in the kingdom, was first made here late in the 18th century. This particular ware is of a fine reddish brown or chocolate colour, and is very smooth and beautiful. The body is of fine, hard and compact white earthenware, and the brown glaze as made by the Bramelds, by which the peculiar shaded and streaky effect was produced, is as fine as it is possible to conceive,

Fig. 84. CADOGAN COFFEE POT. York Museum Collection.

and the goods required to be "dipped" and passed through the firing no fewer than three times before it was considered to be perfect. This is the glaze the recipe for which is in the hands of Mr. Bowman Heald. In its preparation great care is necessary in the selection of the materials, only the very best and purest being used, indeed, when made originally by the Bramelds, they went so far as to use distilled water in the mixings.

Of the many articles made in this charming ware, perhaps the most famous is the curious coffee pot without any lid, and filled from an opening in the bottom of the piece, known as the "Cadogan Pot." This curious piece was formed on the model of an example of green Indian ware, said to have been brought from abroad by the Marquis and Marchioness of Rockingham, or by the Honourable Mrs. Cadogan, and preserved for fifty or sixty

Fig. 85.   PLATE.   Mr. O. Grabham's Collection.

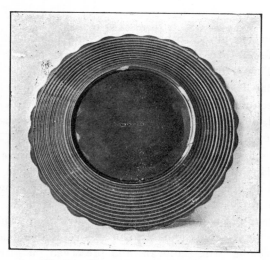

Fig. 86.   UNDERSIDE OF SAME PLATE.

years at Wentworth, before it was thought of being copied. Vessels of this same construction are in existence, which are said to be of early Japanese make. These Rockingham Cadogan pots are said to produce a better flavour of tea and coffee than any others, and were much used by George IV.

The marks used at the Rockingham Works were

*Rockingham* incised on the "Cadogan Pots."

ROCKINGHAM in large and small capitals impressed in the ware, also MORTLOCK and NORFOLK, impressed, Mortlock being the London dealer.

BRAMELD++ in capital letters impressed.

BRAMELD & CO. and BRAMELD in small capital letters impressed.

Mr. T. Boynton tells me that he has seen an early piece of Rockingham or Swinton Ware marked BINGLEY.

The crest of Earl Fitzwilliam—a griffin—was adopted in 1825, on the commencement of the manufacture of china under the assistance of that nobleman, and from that period the pottery was known as the Rockingham Works, instead as heretofore as the Swinton Works.

The griffin is usually painted in red, mauve, or purple, with "Rockingham Works, Brameld," sometimes with the word Royal added, in writing letters in corresponding colour to the griffin, in seven or eight different forms, above, below and around the griffin.

A. Baguley's mark, when he worked at Mexborough, has been described before.

Another mark found on the cane coloured jugs with figures in white in relief upon them, and the upper part of the handle representing the tail of a horse, whilst the lower portion of the same represents a horse's shin and hoof, Fig. 82, is BRAMELD in relief, surrounded by a wreath, all contained in a raised boss or cartouche on the bottom of the jug. One of these pieces is in Mr. Hurst's Collection, and he also has two very curious china extinguishers of Rockingham Ware. These represent the figures of two of the landladies at some of the old country inns. They are well modelled and coloured, and are hollowed out and coloured brown inside, so that they can be used for extinguishing candles.

At Wentworth House, the seat of Earl Fitzwilliam, there is a very fine Collection of Rockingham Ware, and amongst it a magnificent vase, which was the largest china vase produced at at that time in a single piece in this country.   It stands three feet nine inches in height, and is three feet one inch in circumference. The "Dragon Vase" or the "Infernal Vase" was also made, and, according to Jewitt, some of the finest vases which had ever been produced were turned out at these works,

Mr. Freemantle, Barbor Hall, Rotherham, also has a very fine Collection of Rockingham Ware.

Fig. 87.   MARK ON ROCKINGHAM CHINA.

## ROTHERHAM.
## HOLMES POTTERY.

Was started about 1850.   The original proprietors may have been as stated by Jewitt, Messrs Earnshaw and Greaves, but Mr. G. Jarvis built it.   The place was afterwards worked by four partners, Messrs. Jackson, Dickinson, Greaves, and Shaw, from about 1855 to 1870.   From that date to 1880, it was carried on by Mr. G. Shaw, trading as J. Jackson and Co.   Mr. G. Shaw took over the business in 1880, trading as J. Jackson and Co until 1887, when he altered the name of the firm to George Shaw and Sons.

General earthenware is made, white body with printed and other decorations.

Messrs. Shaw tell me that there never has been a trade mark, or any distinctive mark, beyond names of patterns or initials, or the name of the firm, thus, J. J. & Co., up to 1887. From that date, if a mark was used, which was very rarely, it was " G. S. & S."

The patterns principally made here when the pottery started were " Willow," " Wild Rose," etc., and these are still being made.

# ROTHERHAM.
## NORTHFIELD POTTERY.

In 1885, George Hawley purchased Northfield Pottery, Rotherham, from Joseph Lee, who built the works about 1850, and manufactured earthenware for the American markets, the trade mark used being the royal coat of arms.

Prior to building Northfield Pottery, Lee carried on a small pottery near to Bridgegate, Rotherham, which was very primitive but evidently successful, because it enabled him to take up potting on a much larger scale, although within so short a time of his new venture he had to give it up. George Hawley now worked two potteries, namely, Low Pottery, Rawmarsh, and Northfield Pottery, Rotherham, with the assistance of his two sons, William and George, until his death in October 1863. He was a very industrious potter, and was held in the highest esteem by all who knew him, both in business and in private life.

The two sons, William and George succeeded to the business, and continued the manufacture under the style of William and George Hawley, doing a fair amount of export trade as well as supplying the home markets, their trade mark being W. & G. Hawley.

On the death of William, which took place at Rawmarsh in 1868, his three sons, Matthew, the eldest, Walter and Arthur George, took over the Northfield Pottery and carried on as " Hawley Brothers," under the successful management of Matthew, who had always been keenly interested in the business, and who had received a thorough grounding from his father.

George, the surviving brother of William continued at the Low
Pottery, Rawmarsh, trading as "George Hawley." Matthew
Hawley died in August, 1888, leaving his two sons, Sidney and
John William, in partnership in trust with his brother Arthur
George, and it is to Mr. Sidney Hawley that I am indebted for
most of the above information.

In January 1897, the business, for family reasons, was converted
into a private limited liability company, under the name and style
of "Hawley Brothers Ltd.," manufacturing general domestic
earthenware. In the year 1900 leadless glaze was introduced and
used in place of lead glazes, large quantities of goods of a very
fine quality being made for Government use in various departments, besides for railway companies, public institutions, etc.

Fig. 88.   SAUCER.   Mr. O. Grabham's Collection.

In 1903 the Company changed, and at the present time is carried
on as the "Northfield Hawley Pottery Co. Ld.," manufacturing
earthenware of a common kind.

Marked specimens of the Northfield Pottery are rare. We have
a teapot ornamented with curtains and tassels in blue and orange,
having a deep border, at the base, of green leaves on a yellow
ground, with a broad line in dark blue, running at the top and
bottom of the border, impressed HAWLEY on the bottom, and I
have seen a Toby jug similarly marked.

The mark of the Northfield Hawley Pottery Co. Ltd. is a lion rampant, with his right paw placed on a globe. This is on the back of a saucer, decorated on the front with a print of a rural scene in red, in my possession. It is impressed in the ware.

Fig. 89. Impressed Trade Mark of the Factory, and Pattern Mark printed in red, on the Back of the Saucer.

The trade mark of Hawley Brothers consisted of the initials H.B. intertwined in the centre of a shield, and 1790 below them, this being the date when William Hawley founded the Top Pottery, Rawmarsh.

Fig. 90. Teapot. York Museum Collection.

## ROTHWELL POTTERY.

Messrs. J. R. and F. Kidson, in their book on " Leeds Pottery," state that an important pottery was situated here and was a going concern in 1770, doing a considerable trade in earthenware. Wares of all kinds appear to have been manufactured, including cream ware and the ordinary white ware painted in enamel colours.

In 1773 it was in difficulties, and very shortly after was closed down, much of the stock being purchased by the Leeds Pottery.

A new pottery on a smaller scale was started by Samuel Shaw, a potter from Staffordshire, in 1774, but how long he continued to trade is not known, nor is the date of the first establishment of the Rothwell Pottery known.

The field where the pottery formerly stood is now built over, and is known as " Pottery Fold."

## SMALL CLUES POTTERY,

situated at Bradshaw, near Halifax, was commenced between 1800 and 1810 by James Robinson, a dissolving partner from the Catheralls of Soil Hill. It was afterwards worked by a Mr. Wade, and was closed down about 1870. Black ware and the usual " slip " decorated wares of these South Yorkshire potteries were made here.

## SOIL HILL or SWILL HILL POTTERY

is in the township of Ovenden and parish of Halifax, a short distance from the Causeway Foot terminus of the Halifax tramway on the Halifax and Keighley road, under the hill known by the same name, Soil or Swill Hill.

The pottery was started about the year 1770 by one Catherall, and was worked by him and his descendants or connections down to the year 1897, when it passed to Mr. Isaac Button, whose sons still carry it on.

The commencement of Catherall with these local potteries was at Keelham, near Thornton, between 1760 to 1770, by a Jonathan Catherall, then he removed and established the Soil Hill Pottery in 1770. The above Mr. Catherall came from Wales, he was born in 1740 and died in August, 1807. The pottery is also sometimes known as the Swilling End Pottery.

The present buildings were erected in 1898, the old buildings, a little distance away, are in ruins. The clay used, principally common yellow, lies on or near the surface in varying depths. Common articles such as plant pots, washing bowls, bread and stew pots, troughs, with some fancy and rustic ware such as hen and chicken money boxes, cuckoos, etc., as well as puzzle jugs or teasing pitchers, are the articles made here.

There is no distinctive mark or initials on the ware, and specimens of the early work are very bad to get hold of.

Through the kindness of Mr. Nicholas Taylor, late of the Denholme Pottery, I obtained several interesting pieces for our

Collection, decorated in yellow slip, with initials and dated, such as a flower pot, knife box, holder for a pound of candles, sugar box, etc.   These decorated pieces were the work of a Samuel Catherall, who worked at the Soil Hill Pottery, he died about 1887.   None of these West Riding potteries used a trade mark, and the different makes can only be distinguished by their glaze, colour of body and decorations.   Soil Hill about 1867 did most of the quill stringing and decorations in relief.   Howcans and Denholme did a portion also.   Mostly prints in relief were done at Howcans.   Inlaying was done at all of them.

Fig. 91.   HOLDER FOR A POUND OF TALLOW CANDLES.
York Museum Collection.

On a highly ornamented flower pot in this ware in our Collection, with the pot itself and the stand for the same ringed round with small handles, is this inscription in incised letters, " S. C. Born March 19th, 1807, and made this pot April 29th, 1868, at Swilling End."

The initials stand for the Samuel Catherall mentioned above. We also have a fine knife box, differing from the Howcans one in being quite solid along the sides, not with open trellis work that exists in the Howcans piece.   It is decorated with masks in relief, and bears the date 1872.

G

# STOCKTON-ON-TEES.

## THE STAFFORD POTTERY.

There were several potteries at Stockton, but only one on the Yorkshire or south side of the river Tees, known as the Stafford Pottery, at Thornaby-on-Tees. It was established in 1825 by Mr. William Smith, and began as a small brown ware pottery, but the founder, a man of energy and enterprize, roused to emulation by the thriving potteries on the Wear, determined to enlarge his scheme of operations. He went into Staffordshire and there engaged a managing partner. Mr. John Whalley, who had an intimate knowledge of potting, gained in some of the best known Staffordshire works. In 1826 the firm began operations under the style of William Smith and Co. In order to get command of more capital Messrs. William and George Skinner were taken into partnership, and eventually the firm became George Skinner and Co. On Mr. Whalley's retirement, Mr. Ambrose Walker, a native of Hanley but an inhabitant of Stockton from his boyhood, who had also the advantage of having been trained under Mr. Whalley, and who had received from him all his valuable recipes, etc., undertook the management, and the firm became Skinner and Walker in 1870.

The Stafford Pottery was noted for the extensive use of machinery at a time when the art of " throwing" was almost entirely a manual labour.

At one time a branch pottery was established at Genappes, near Mons, in Belgium, the workmen being sent over from Stockton. The pottery still continues, being carried on by the Thornaby Pottery Co. Ltd., and employs about one hundred hands.

The wares made are common printed and sponged earthenware and the brown ware, often called "Sunderland" ware, because it was first made at that town. It is made from the natural clay of the district, and has a lining or "slip" applied to the inside, while the outside is left of the natural colour and glazed almost to the bottom. It has been one of the industrial products of the County of Durham for the past 120 years.

Cane ware is also made from clay the colour of bamboo or thereabouts. It is very unusual for it to have any coloured decoration, though often "slipt" white or blue inside.

In 1848 an injunction was granted against the firm at the instance of the Wedgwoods, of Etruria, for the infringement of patent, the Stockton firm using the name Wedgwood in their mark, generally wrongly spelt with the addition of an E, thus:

W. S. & Co's. WEDGEWOOD, impressed.

Another mark adopted by the firm, also impressed on the bottom of the ware, was

W. S. & Co's.

QUEEN'S WARE.

Some pieces have elaborate printed marks. The name of the pattern, fruit basket and garland, with W. S. & Co., and in addition the number and W. S. & Co's., impressed.

Mr. Hurst has a plate having on the back the forged Wedgwood mark, WEDGEWOOD, impressed, and on the rim of the plate also at the back, enclosed in scrolls, all being in black transfer:

W. S. & CO.

## Stafford Pottery

### No. 16.

Plates were made here with German mottoes on them for export to Germany.

The mugs with the picture of the No. 1 engine and carriages on it were made here, but were doubtless made at other potteries as

Fig. 92. RAILWAY MUG SHOWING No. 1. ENGINE. York Museum Collection.

Fig. 93.   RAILWAY MUG.   York Museum Collection.

Fig. 94.   RAILWAY MUG.   York Museum Collection.

Fig. 95.   RAILWAY MUG.   Mr. J. R. Triffitt's Collection..

well, as it would be a popular subject for such a purpose, 80 or 90 years ago. The engine depicted on the mug in our Collection, namely, the Express, was that which ran between Liverpool and Manchester about 1827—1830. The engines bore the names of some of the old horse coaches, such as the "Tally-ho," "High-flier," "Mail," "Eclipse," etc. Some of the nobility and gentry through whose land the line passed had the privilege of having one of their carriages strapped on to the top of the last plain flat-topped railway wagon, and of riding in it if they did not care to go in the ordinary coaches. In our mug the carriage on the last wagon is empty, but on one belonging to Mr. J. R. Triffitt, a whole family is shown sat in the carriage, ladies and gentlemen, and a man perched in the "dickey" behind, the luggage being placed on the top of the preceding coach.

As recently as 1914 I find that the Great Eastern Railway Co. stated in their time tables that "passengers riding in their own carriages are charged first class fare." This was kindly pointed out to me by Mr. J. W. Davis, York.

Fig. 96. PLATE. Mr. O. Grabham's Collection.

The pretty blue and white and brown and white marbled and combed chargers or dishes, some of them of large size, and known as "Welsh trays," though why I have never been able to discover, were *not* made at the Stafford Pottery, but only at the "Clarence Potteries," Norton, on the Durham side of the Tees. They were much in vogue for about thirty years, beginning in 1850, but the demand for them gradually dwindled down to nothing, and none were made here since 1895. They were chiefly used by butchers as meat dishes and are now somewhat difficult to obtain.

Only the early ones were marked HARWOOD, impressed on the back. The colouring or combing on some of these dishes is on the top of the glaze and not under it.

Some fine cobles, in pottery, were made at Stockton. These are representations of the Yorkshire fishing and pleasure boats known as cobles. Also toad and frog mugs, decorated with lustre and a verse and a ship outside, and having the usual amphibian inside.

Fig. 97.   COBLE.   Mr. A. Hurst's Collection.

Fig. 98.   TOAD MUG.   York Museum Collection.

The other potteries in Stockton, though on the Durham side of the Tees, were the "**Clarence Potteries,**" **Norton,** where the Welsh trays were made, founded by Thomas Harwood in 1849, and carried on by him till his death. Sold by his trustees in 1877 to the present owners and operators, " The Clarence Potteries Co.

Ltd," and it is to Mr. P. Graham, of the above firm, that I am indebted for much of the information concerning them.

**Old Clarence Pottery, Stockton.** Founded in 1825 by Thomas Harwood, and subsequently carried on by his sons as "Harwood Brothers" and others, and demolished about 1887. Only Sunderland ware was made here, and no special mark was ever used.

**Stockton Pottery, Stockton, Ainsworth's.** Founded in the forties by Thomas Ainsworth, and closed down and demolished in 1901. The mark used was the Stockton coat of arms, namely, an anchor and cable impaling a castle, impressed in the ware.

**North Shore Pottery, Smith's,** was demolished about 1888. Last carried on by Wm. Smith, a son of the founder, who, after leaving Stockton, started Cliffe House Pottery, West Hartlepool. This pottery was demolished about 1898. I have a plate marked G. F. S. (George Fothergill Smith).

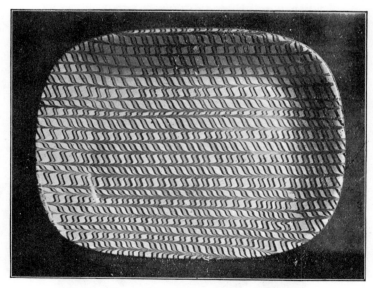

Fig. 99. WELSH TRAY. York Museum Collection.

## SWILLINGTON BRIDGE POTTERY.

Situated near Methley, in a field adjoining the river Aire and the bridge which spans the same, very little is known about this pottery. The 1845 Survey marks a pottery of black ware near Swillington Bridge. It is said to have been closed owing to the smoke from the fires blowing across the Lowther's park. Large trees now grow over part of the site, and very few people know that a pottery ever existed here.

Specimens of this ware are very rare. We have the only marked piece that I have ever seen. It was most kindly presented to us by Mr. J. R. Kidson, of 116 Albion Street, Leeds. It is a round plaque, with figures in relief in colours, and incised on the back, "John Wildblood Swillington Bridge Pottery, July 12th, 1831."

Mr. Thomas Boynton has a big jug but it is unmarked, and Mr. A. Hurst has a large two-handled loving cup, also not marked, with this inscription on it, between two lines of painted flowers:

> "Eshaldwell Brewery is known very well
> For brewing good ale none it can excel
> Pay off your old scores and order again
> For im sure of the ale you cannot complain.

Fig. 100. PLAQUE. York Museum Collection.

## WOODLESFORD POTTERY.

I have, unfortunately, not been able to ascertain when this pottery was first started. It was working in 1845 under the firm of Gibson and Shackleton. Then Benjamin Taylor had it, and the last proprietors were Messrs. Hewitt and Jenkinson.

It closed down as an eathenware pottery in 1891, but was worked as a fine art pottery for two or three years later.

There were three kilns, but only common household ware, such as pots, dinner services, etc., were made. No marks were used, except the names of the patterns on the back of some of the pieces, such as " Willow," " Eton College," etc.

We have a sauce-boat of this ware, for which, along with the information given above, I am indebted to Mr. Benjamin Walker, of 10 Church Street, Woodlesford, who worked at the pottery for about thirty years, starting in 1857, at the age of fourteen.

## WOODNAM HOUSE POTTERY.

Situated at Elland, and also known as Blackley Pottery, was changed into a black ware from a fine ware pottery between 1860 and 1870 by Titus Kitson, whose father, Joseph Kitson, was a potter previously just above Woodnam House Pottery. Then he, Joseph Kitson, removed, and commenced at Ainley Top Pottery, about 1839. This was closed down about 1886. These Kitsons have been established as potters since 1820.

Woodnam House Pottery was worked as a fine ware pottery in the 18th century by a Mr. Cartledge, and a piece of this ware is now in the possession of Mr. Titus Kitson, junr., dated 1734. We also have a crude jug of this ware dated 1719, standing on three very short legs, brown glaze, decorated with light yellow slip, also a much later photograph frame with the inscription: THINK OF ME. Woodnam House Pottery was closed in 1907.

## YEARSLEY POTTERY.

At Yearsley, near Coxwold, there was a pottery in early times, which is especially interesting, because one branch of the Wedg-woods of Staffordshire settled there at an early date. There is in the museum attached to the Abbey at Ampleforth a large cistern, covered with the old green glaze, having on it, in incised letters, John Wedg Wood which was made here, which the authorities at Ampleforth Abbey most kindly allowed me to examine and photograph ; and Jewitt mentions a puzzle jug which used to be in the Museum of Practical Geology, London, having the same name on it, and the date 1691, in the same green lead glaze which was made here.

Fig. 101. CISTERN. Ampleforth Abbey Museum.

A John Wedgwood made pots in Walmgate, York, in the beginning of the 18th century.

The ware made by the Yorkshire Wedgwoods was the common hard brown ware made from the clays of the district, and consisted mainly of pitchers, pancheons, porringers, and other vessels of a homely kind.

One member of the Wedgwood family has been immortalized in song,

" At Yearsley there are pancheons made,
By Willie Wedgwood, that young blade."

Pancheons are thick coarse earthenware pans, made of various sizes, and used for setting away milk in, and for washing purposes. They are made in many localities, and besides being sold by earthenware dealers, are hawked about the country by men who make their living in no other way. Several fragments of brown pottery have been dug up at Yearsley, and amongst the rest, Jewitt mentions a brown earthenware oven, green glaze, semicircular, open at the top, with a hollowed ledge round the inner side about half way, and a flat bottom, having two handles at the sides, and between them a crinkled ornament bearing some letters, and the date 1712.

The Yearsley Pottery has been done away with for many years, and now the plough goes over its site. I have found several fragments of the old pottery when going over the ground.

## YORK.   PLACE'S   WARE.

The names of potters appear very early in the list of the Freemen of York. The first to be mentioned is Thomas de Brandesby, potter, in the 12th year of the reign of Edward the First, 1284.

Fig. 102.   Jug.   Mr. T. Boynton's Collection.

Francis Place, who may be looked upon as one of the pioneers of modern pottery, commenced the manufacture of what at the

time was considered " equal to true china ware," about the year
1665.  But little is known however either of the manufactory or
of the ware he produced.  The former is supposed to have been
situated somewhere on the site of the King's Manor, now the Blind
School, but though I have often made enquiries, I have never been
able to hear of any fragments ever having been found there when
excavations were going on.  Of the latter, one piece of the ware,
originally in the possession of Horace Walpole, namely, a coffee
cup, is now in the British Museum, and a jug is in the Collection
of Mr. Thomas Boynton, of Bridlington, and one or two more
pieces are said to be in the hands of some of his descendants, but
the ware is of extreme rarity.  It was simply a tolerably fine kind
of earthenware, of a greyish colour streaked with black and brown.
Place was an artist of some merit, and designed and etched.

Thoresby in his " Ducatus Leodinensis " (1714) mentions Place
and his wares several times, and Walpole says : " His pottery cost
him much money ; he attempted it solely from a turn for experiments, but one Clifton took the hint from him, and made a fortune
by it."  *Vide* Ferrybridge Pottery.

## YORK  CHINA  MANUFACTORY.

In 1838 Mr. Haigh Hirstwood, formerly of the Rockingham
China Works, established a china manufactory in York, and by
the succeeding spring had so far progressed that the following
paragraph appeared in one of the York papers : " York China
Manufactory—Mr. Hirstwood, of Stonegate, is erecting a kiln,
extensive warehouses. etc., in the Groves, for manufacturing,
gilding, and burnishing china. which has not previously been
attempted in this city."

The works were established in Lowther Street, Groves, and
were continued until about 1850, when the concern was wound
up.  Mr. Haigh Hirstwood was at the famous Rockingham works,
under the Bramelds, for forty years, he was a clever painter of
flowers, etc., and was considered the best fly painter at the
Rockingham works.

According to Jewitt, in 1826 he copied for use in the decoration
of the Rockingham china upwards of five hundred insects at
Wentworth House, which had been arranged by Lady Milton,
the daughter-in-law of Earl Fitzwilliam.  He, and his sons Joseph
and Thomas, who were brought up at the Rockingham works,

were engaged upon the *chefs-d'œuvre* of that manufactory, namely, the services for King William IV. and for the Duchess of Cumberland. He was succeeded in his business in Coney Street, where the china, etc., was sold, by his son William Hirstwood, who was not a practical potter like Joseph and Thomas.

When Haigh Hirstwood started kilns in Lowther Street and commenced business in the decorating and finishing departments, he did not actually make any, but bought his china, etc., in the "white" from Sampson, Bridgwood, and Co., of Longton, Staffordshire, and from others, and then decorated and finished it. He was assisted in his work by his son-in-law, William Leyland, who was also from the Rockingham works, and a clever painter, gilder, and enameller, but disagreements arose and the partnership was dissolved, Mr. Hirstwood dying in York in 1854. Mr. Leyland removed to London, where he took to printing and decorating lamps, and he died there in 1853. No special mark was used by Hirstwood.

The Misses Hoyle, Gillygate, York, grand-daughters of Haigh Hirstwood, have two plaques painted by Joseph Hirstwood, representing various flowers such as roses, dahlias, tulips, auriculas, woody nightshade, etc., and one painted by William Leyland showing foxglove, moss rose, guelder rose, and tulip. These are beautifully done, and I am much indebted to the Misses Hoyle for much information, and also for being permitted to examine their plaques and to have them photographed.

They very kindly presented us with a broken plate, painted by Joseph Hirstwood, representing a basket of grapes, cherries, strawberries, currants, etc., with a broad blue border, having gilt bands and edge. Miss Sarah Hoyle remembers breaking this when she was a little girl. It is in the Rockingham style.

It is not known where the Jonathan Martin mugs were made. They represent on one side Jonathan Martin with heavy fetters on either side of him, and this inscription : " Jonathan Martin, the Incendiary, Tried March 31st, 1829, before Mr. Baron Hullock, and sentenced to confinement during His Majesty's pleasure."

On the other side is a picture of the Minster burning, and this inscription : " York Minster on fire, Feby. 2nd, 1829." These mugs are very rarely to be obtained now. We have one in blue transfer, and Mr. E. J. Hardcastle, York, has one in the same colour. We also have one in black transfer, smaller than that in blue.

Fig. 103.   PLAQUE PAINTED BY JOSEPH HIRSTWOOD.
The Misses Hoyle's Collection.

Fig. 104.   PLAQUE PAINTED BY WILLIAM LEYLAND.
The Misses Hoyle's Collection.

I have a blue printed earthenware soup plate which has printed on the back in large ornamental capitals in blue,

## J. T. BUCKLE & CO. YORK.

In 1846, John Townsend Buckle & Co., 18 Low Ousegate, York, were china and earthenware merchants. The firm is now Messrs. Newington and Scott.

Mr. Giles, the deputy town clerk of York, tells me that he has found Mansion House accounts with Buckle and Co. in 1842 for the sum of two pounds, six shillings, and in 1845 for the sum of forty-four pounds, eight shillings, for china, etc. The white china cups and saucers at the Mansion House, York, with a broad blue band, and the York coat of arms in the centre in colours, were made by Messrs. Minton, but the saucers have on the back in writing letters, J. T. Buckle & Co. York.

It was often the practice for dealers in china and earthenware to have their names put on the ware they dealt in, though of course they had nothing whatever to do with the manufacture of the same, which was turned out for them at some well-known pottery.

The Registered Mark Act only came into force about 1867, though of course many potteries adopted marks of their own long before that. Pieces marked according to the Act may be about 1867 or much later, for once on the register the makers generally use the mark on their ware.

There are preserved at the Mansion House some very interesting Ward cups, generally known as the " Ward Pottery," but they are in reality made of porcelain, and, in the opinion of Mr. J. R. Kidson, Leeds, are Salopian ware, made at the Caughley factory in Shropshire, in the latter half of the 18th century.

These cups are white, with a dark blue and gilt rim, and bear the coat of arms of the city of York, viz.: *argent* a cross *gules* charged with five lions passant and guardant *or*, also, according to the particular Ward to which they belong, the words

## MICKLE GATE WARD.
## MONCK WARD.
## WALMGATE WARD.
### Bootham WARD.

The Bootham cups have the lettering smaller than on the others, and they are without the blue and gilt rim. When Mr. Rhodes Brown was Lord Mayor in 1913, he very kindly allowed me to carefully examine all the cups, and have a specimen from each

Fig. 105. YORK WARD CUPS.

Fig, 106. YORK WARD CUPS.

Fig. 107. YORK WARD CUPS.

Fig. 108. YORK WARD CUPS.

Ward photographed. In 1915 the then Lord Mayor, Mr. J. Bowes Morrell and the Corporation, most kindly loaned to us one cup from each of the four Wards to be exhibited in our fine Collection of Yorkshire Pottery. When I examined the cups in 1913 there were of Bootham Ward 16, Micklegate Ward 17, Monck Ward 13, Walmgate Ward 18.

These cups were used for drinking burnt wine, etc., in, and I am indebted to Mr. T. P. Cooper, York, for the following, which is of considerable interest :

The

Customs and Orders

Of the

Lord Mayor

Aldermen, Sheriffs, Four-and-

Twenty, and Commons

of the

City of York

touching

The wearing of their several Gowns, and

the several Treats or Entertainments at

Elections and Admittance into Council

and other Antient Customs.

York :

Printed by A. Ward, in Coney Street

1762.

" Treats at the Common Hall." "At the election of Lord Mayor, 12 gallons of red and white wine : whereof 5 gallons in the inner Room, and 6 gallons to the commoners (to be divided equally amongst the Wards), and 1 gallon to the chamberlains, six shillingsworth of White Manchet Half-penny Rolls ; whereof four dozen of Rolls to the commoners : viz. one Dozen to every Ward, and the rest to the inner Room. Two table-cloths, and six napkins in the inner Room : a Pound and a Half of refined Loaf Sugar, 24 Cups for burnt Wine, two Tea Kettles for burning it, and 24 Drinking Glasses for cold wine, at the expense of the Person elected ; and Wine and Sugar in Tankards and 2 Biscuits for each member that sets the Lord Mayor elect, home."

At the election of Alderman and Sheriffs, similar drinks, etc., were provided, also Cups : 24 Plates, Pipes and Tobacco were provided when Aldermen were sworn.

H

## YORK.  LAYERTHORPE POTTERY

was established in 1846 by Mr. John Webster, the ware made consisting of flower pots, chimney pots, bowls, socket pipes, etc. It was closed down between forty and fifty years ago.

Many other small potteries existed throughout the County, such as those at Osmotherley, Wakefield Moor, Potovens, near Wakefield, Rosedale, etc.

———◆———

So many people are unacquainted with the legend of the popular " Willow " pattern, which is and has been so largely used to decorate various pieces of pottery, both the typical pattern, here reproduced, and its variations, that I make no apology for introducing it here. I am very much indebted to Mr. H. M. Loadman, Stonegate, York, for the loan of the blocks of the frontispiece— which is Mr. Loadman's own idea of the York " Willow " pattern —and for the typical " Willow " here reproduced.

### STORY OF THE " WILLOW " PATTERN.

In the house seen on the right hand side of the plate lived a Mandarin who wished his daughter Li-Chi to marry an old but wealthy suitor.  Knowing that she was loved by Chang, his secretary, he imprisoned her in a room overlooking the water, so the lady sent a message in a cocoa nut shell floating down the stream, arranging to meet Chang when the Willow leaf began to fall.  This he received, and by the help of a gardener who lived in the small house under the fir tree, the lovers met and are seen fleeing away over the bridge, the lady in front, Chang following with her jewel case, and the Mandarin pursuing them with a whip. But they escaped in the boat to an island where they lived happily until discovered by the wealthy suitor, who, in revenge, set fire to the house.  Their prayers for help being heard, they were changed into the two birds seen flying away safe, under the protection of the gods.

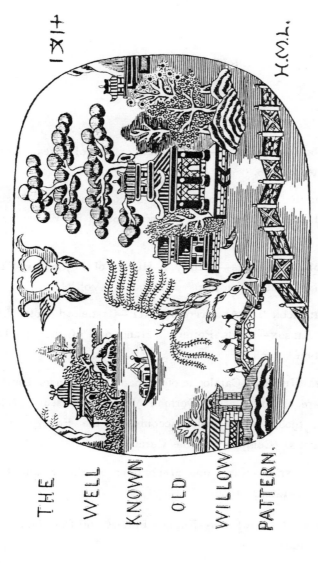

Fig. 109. The "Willow" Pattern.

# BIBLIOGRAPHY.

———— ⊷•⊷ ————

LLEWELLYNN JEWITT—The Ceramic Art of Great Britain. Illustrated. 1878.

JOSEPH R. KIDSON AND FRANK KIDSON—Historical Notices of the Old Leeds Pottery, with a description of its Wares. Illustrated. 1892.

DR. MAUD SELLERS—Pottery, A History of the County of York. (Victoria County Histories). Illustrated. Vol. II. 1912.

ARCHDEACON H. ARMSTRONG HALL—Castleford Pottery, and FRANK KIDSON—Leeds Pottery. Handbook of the old Leeds Exhibition. 1908.

BAKER HUDSON—Catalogue of a Loan Collection of Linthorpe Art Ware, exhibited at the Dorman Memorial Museum, Middlesbrough, 1906, with a brief account of the Pottery and its productions. Compiled by the Curator.

W. CHAFFERS—Marks and Monograms on Pottery and Porcelain. Illustrated. 1906.

E. WARD A. DOWNMAN—English Pottery and Porcelain. Illustrated. 1904.